THE RISE OF

MODERN COMMUNISM

A Brief History of the Communist
Movement in the Twentieth Century

MASSIMO SALVADORI

HENRY HOLT AND COMPANY New York

36429

Contents

Introduction

Massimo Salvadori has put us all deeply in his debt by writing this brief, concise, and perceptive story of the rise of modern communism. It fills a very deep need. So far as I know there is nothing in English which covers the same ground so briefly and so comprehensively. I imagine that many students of communism might, like myself, prefer some changes in emphasis or wording in dealing with highly controversial material. But I predict that most of them will join me in praise of the author's learning, objectivity of approach, and standards of social value.

The book is the more welcome because we Americans are in a position of passionately opposing a movement which we do not understand. Indeed the passion of our opposition is comparatively recent. During World War II and for about a year thereafter we enjoyed something like a honeymoon with Stalin. I never heard him so highly praised by any non-communist as by Wendell Willkie, titular leader of the Republican party, after the latter had discovered "one world." (Therein lies a lesson that no one should quote any man's opinion of Russia or communism without giving the date.)

Now, however, public opinion has swung to total opposition to communism. By no means are we mistaken in our purpose of resisting it and its relentless drive to power. But many of our reasons for opposing communism are based on an ignorant or willful misunderstanding of its nature. Too many of us are like a physician who, aware that his patient is sick, treats him for typhus when he should treat him for typhoid. Or we are like a general who fights an enemy concerning whose forces and their disposition his scouts give him inaccurate and widely divergent information.

In recent months, at one extreme, I have heard communism described as merely "the sum of democracy's mistakes," merely "the natural product of the world's bitter economic inequality" and of "the hunger of half of its inhabitants." At an opposite extreme, communism is described as "gangsterism, writ large," the "invention of the devil" with no appeal except through force. One of the most popular definitions of communism is "socialism in a hurry." There is even an equation, dear to many propagandists, which goes like this, "Trumanism equals socialism equals communism." Some differences may be admitted but they are temporary and unimportant. The welfare state is, these extremists say, the first stage of communism.

Usually by the would-be literate, communism is described as the natural and almost inevitable expression of Marxism. Marx, Lenin, and Stalin are indiscriminately lumped together. The novelist, Louis Bromfield, suddenly turned sociological as well as agricultural expert, recently wrote: "Socialism and Communism derive from exactly the same source, a shrewd, psychopathic, neurotic barbarian named Karl Marx, a product of Central Europe which has never known democracy in any form."

I, who am not a Marxist, would challenge the description of Marx as a barbarian or as the product of a region that never knew any democracy. He was in the strictest sense a Westerner, who had lived through the liberal movements of the early nineteenth century and did most of his writing in London where he lies buried.

We shall get absolutely nowhere in our fight against communism by failing to realize the historical complexities of the situation which gave birth to Marxism and its development along different lines: anarcho-syndicalist, democratic socialist, and communist. In the process there were many elements introduced, not derived, from Marx. It is one of Mr. Salvadori's many virtues that he brings this out so clearly in his discussion of the rise of modern communism.

Unquestionably, that movement owes much to Marxism which nevertheless it distorted in important particulars. Unquestionably, its success has been due not merely to poverty but to a growing apprehension that poverty is unnecessary and that the extremes of economic inequality in the world are indefensible. Nevertheless, these factors by spontaneous generation never gave rise of themselves to communism. Communism is a secular religion. It is held devoutly by men and women, not recruited from the proletariat, to whom faith in communism is a "character response," as Mr. Salvadori well describes it. As a character response, it appeals to those who feel the need of discipline and of authoritarian support even if it is the support of chains. On the other hand, in other individuals or sometimes in the same individuals, it appeals to the desire for power, perhaps a messianic power to set things right, to be asserted less by individual strength than by a rigorously disciplined elite.

When Mr. Salvadori enumerates the principal doctrines of Marx and then later the principal doctrines of Lenin and the sources of his power, and finally catalogues the strengths and weaknesses of communism, he performs an invaluable service for confused Americans. One may argue this or that point and yet agree that the author has shown balanced judgment in analyzing mighty forces.

It is not our author's business specifically to apply the lessons he teaches about communism to the cold war against it, but his contribution to our understanding is so great that I should like to elaborate certain lessons implicit in what he has written. As everybody knows, I write as a democratic socialist. But I am not arguing the merits of socialism when I point out the great danger to success in democracy's struggle against communism which lies in the current attempt to identify socialism with communism. What makes communism a universal danger is its relentless drive for power over the bodies and minds and souls of men. This drive for power is by no means derived purely and inescapably from the economics of social ownership.

I could argue from the record that communist economics have become the economics of a police state capitalism, a betrayal of the socialist desire for democratic controls of the economic process for the good of all. I prefer at this point to emphasize the fact that a high degree of economic collectivism could coexist in the world alongside the fluid capitalism of the United States. (Really we already have one variety of a mixed economy.) The American and the communist economies might at times clash and mutually influence each other. Of themselves they would not drive the world to the madness of the arms economy or the greater madness of war. It is the totalitarian drive for power that is dangerous.

That drive has been emphatically rejected by the democratic socialists of the world. And that not merely in words. Great Britain and the Scandinavian countries, in which socialist governments have held office, have been scrupulous to preserve democratic institutions and civil liberties. The ancient jest that the difference between socialism and communism is five years is completely refuted by the fact that in these countries, socialist parties have held office for more than five years without trying to establish one-party systems or to abridge free elections and free campaigns.

At present it suits powerful interests to argue various economic questions in America on the assumption that welfare measures must lead to communism and that communism is bad. Enough welfare measures have already been adopted, and enough security of employment has been afforded by the arms economy, to keep the mass of the workers temporarily content and quiescent under torrents of propaganda concerning the supposed conquest of poverty in America. The plain truth, however, is that we had chronic depression in the United States from October 1929 until Pearl Harbor and that full employment has been the child of war and now of rearmament. There are plenty of unsolved economic problems in America which sooner or later will have to be faced on their merits. It will be hard to argue them fairly if masses of people have been indoctrinated by the notion that the advocacy of public health measures or ample provisions for housing is communistic. They may say, then, that communism can't be so bad. Meanwhile, the difficult business of keeping a good working alliance between the United States and western Europeans is seriously complicated by the sweeping condemnation of all democratic socialist parties in Great Britain, Belgium, Holland, Scandinavian countries, and Western Germany. Democracy does not fight totalitarianism when it finds it easier to accept Franco in Spain than Bevan or even Attlee in Britain.

Another very important and controversial question on which Mr. Salvadori's study sheds light is that of American government's responsibility for communist success in China. Mr. Salvadori's well-phrased analysis allows for American mistakes, but to the discerning reader it should be clear that if every one of Senator McCarthy's reckless charges against the State Department were to be proved true, they would still afford an insufficient explanation of the revolutionary change by means of which communism captured a nation of 400,000,000 people who until recently lived under the oldest and most conservative culture on this earth.

I do not mean to imply in what I have written that Mr. Salvadori is committed by his analysis of communism and its rise to the precise policies which I should recommend in fighting it. I merely say that he gives us a factual background with sufficient interpretation of facts to enable us to argue policies intelligently on the basis of a factual reality which is lacking in most of our torrents of words in print and over the air waves.

It is something of a triumph that the author had needed no more pages to do so good a job. In discovering the anatomy of communism, we need to get at its skeleton. We need to understand its growth in terms of broad basic principles and major historical events. Yet I hope that the reader of this book will want to carry his studies of modern communism farther. Here Mr. Salvadori has given us help in his well-selected bibliography.

In his condensed narrative he has made only one omission which, from the standpoint of his purpose, I am inclined to regret. And that is by no means a complete omission. He mentions the existence of forced labor in communist societies, but with too little emphasis. It is one of the most powerful instrumentalities by which a ruthless dictatorship grinds men into submission. It is also more than that. It has become an essential part of the Soviet economy, a factor in the industrialization and militarization of mighty Russia.

And yet to multitudes in Asia and even in Europe, communism still appears as a form of emancipation. Some weeks ago, Arnold Toynbee, the famous British historian, over the British Broadcasting Corporation made a remarkable address. He personified Russia as telling the Asian nations that once she had been a poor peasant country, exploited by her own rulers and by the West, even as the Asian lands are exploited today. By communism she had lifted herself up to her present position of comparative prosperity and great power.

That sort of appeal is profoundly effective in Asian lands. In three different Indian cities, different sorts of people told me that they did not like communism but that India would have to go communist, because only communism could discipline her for industrialization and enable her people to accumulate working capital out of their already empty stomachs. An Indian leader, openly sympathetic with the democracies of the West, quoted Toynbee's address in full to a gathering here in America as explaining the appeal of communists. One answer to that appeal lies in far wider dissemination of the facts about forced labor. It is the re-institution of chattel slavery on an immense scale, this time to the state, under communist imperial power.

The other and even more essential answer must lie in a democratic program for dealing cooperatively with the problem of poverty. The communist missionary never appears in Asian, African, or Latin American countries outside the iron curtain as the preacher of communist power. He appears sincerely as the advocate of justice and opportunity for exploited peasants and workers. Mao was first of all an agrarian reformer in China, even while he was a communist, and such is the nature of human psychology that it is not necessary to believe that he and his devoted followers were nothing but hypocrites exploiting misery in order to establish their own tyranny. They were dealing with real evil and it will never do for us, the protagonists of democracy, simply to parrot the truth that in the end the communist tyranny is worse than any which it dispossesses. We must offer a way of hope to the hungry multitudes.

I have lived through the years in which the communist movement has grown to power. I once rejoiced in the bolshevik revolution as a great milestone in human progress. I have tried to cooperate with communists and have fought with communists. I never accepted the communist god who failed many an idealist believer. But I have known the pain and disillusionment of seeing socialism distorted and betrayed by the followers of Lenin. For me, reading Mr. Salvadori's book was an emotional experience. Many of his calm, summary sentences brought before my eyes vivid pictures of past events and stirred again the sorrow of hopes betrayed. And those hopes were passionately shared by multitudes in many lands.

Today I can imagine no greater catastrophe than the universal triumph of communism. It would not bring the abject peace of universal slavery. Rather more than the author, I am inclined to believe that the inevitable rivalries for power in a universal communist empire would soon drench the world in blood. Tito's revolt seems to me a foretaste of what will come. But first a universal communism could put out the lights of freedom and justice all over the world. Liberty and democracy would not soon grow again in the sterile soil of hate and hunger. George Orwell, in his famous satire, *1984,* had prophetic vision when, for the first time in literature, he made the utopia toward which we drift obviously a place of horror. He was equally prophetic when he saw not one universal totalitarian empire, but three continually struggling with one another, because each of their dictators needed an enemy to help him maintain his regime at home.

If we are to prevent such a terrible apocalypse for mankind as Mr. Orwell has pictured, it will be in part because the democracies have an understanding of communism which they now lack. To this understanding, Mr. Salvadori has greatly contributed.

Norman Thomas

January 1, 1952

1

From the Origins to the End of the First Phase of the Comintern

SOCIALISM, like other contemporary movements which originated in Europe, is better understood when seen against the background of European liberalism (similar although not equivalent to democracy in American terminology). Liberal parties were the main political expression of the aspiration toward liberty that animated the dynamic minorities of most European nations during the nineteenth century. By the last quarter of the century these movements had seemingly become the dominant element in most aspects of European life.

European liberalism was based on individualism, on the assumption that man, being endowed with reason, can be responsible for his self-determined actions. It postulated the freeing of the individual from political and intellectual bondage, and the establishment of polities which would favor the untrammeled expression of the individual personality. Liberalism achieved success first in Great Britain, later on the Continent and among the offshoots of European nations in other parts of the world.

For several generations liberalism, individualism, and rationalism gave direction to the innumerable changes produced in Europe by the freeing of individual energies. Liberalism led to the abolition of slavery, serfdom, and other restrictions on personal liberty; to the emphasis on what Europeans call the Rights of Man and Americans call Civil Liberties; to the recognition of the moral equality of

1

men. Political liberalism found its expression in parliamentarian institutions, based at first on limited, later—after it had incorporated the democratic trend—on universal suffrage; it stressed the division of powers as the means of eliminating arbitrary actions and of consolidating the rule of law; it emphasized government by consent and by discussion. In the economic field, liberalism—through its stress on private ownership of property, on the individual's right to do what he likes with his property, and on free trade—fostered the advance of capitalism and the greatest expansion of economic activities ever witnessed by human societies. In the realm of ideas, liberalism found its main expression in a broad variety of conceptual frameworks, all based on a rational approach to man and man's problems; it weakened the traditional pressure of dogmatic religious beliefs, and provided a fertile ground for the development of modern science and for the birth of new ideas (many of which were antagonistic to liberalism itself). Among the peoples of Europe it produced nationalism—that is, the emphasis on national liberty or independence.

During the period of liberal ascendancy, physical and mental bonds had sometimes been destroyed, or at least weakened. By the end of the nineteenth century, if we consider Europe alone, progress, under conditions of expanding freedom, had been rapid. This was true both for the countries where liberalism had been most successful (Great Britain, France, the smaller northwestern nations), and for those where it was still struggling, with varying success, against monarchical or aristocratic despotism, militarism, and clericalism (the nations of the southern peninsulas, the empires of central and eastern Europe). Rapid also had been the increase in dissatisfaction, connected with the abrupt changes undergone by citizens of every nation. Economic changes particularly were causing much suffering. Europeans were considerably less poor around 1900 than they had been a century earlier, but they were more conscious of their poverty and freer to express feelings of discontent. There was less injustice, but greater consciousness of what injustice remained.

The widespread anti-liberal and anti-individualistic re-action which acquired impetus at the end of the nineteenth century was directed either against liberalism as a whole or against one or more of the elements with which it had become identified at one time or another. Liberalism was denied *in toto* by those who found inspiration in the values and institutions of the pre-liberal period, and also by integral nationalists, racists, and others. Among those who accepted some of the fundamental principles of liberalism but rejected others, the socialists formed the largest group.

The early socialists were French and British. They became vocal in the 1820's when they shared the liberals' hatred for political despotism and for intellectual obscurantism. They maintained, however, that the evils which had accompanied the growth of liberalism could be corrected only by curbing individualism and by making society responsible for the triumph of justice. Instead of capitalism they advocated collectivism, varying from social ownership and management of some basic industries to the socialization of all economic activities. Instead of nationalism they advocated internationalism. Instead of free movement within a population differentiated economically, politically, and culturally, they advocated the elimination of differentiation. The liberals had aimed at emasculating the state; the socialists, although often talking of the ultimate elimination of the state, were led to strengthen its authority in order to curb the differences which develop within a free society.

One of the important results of the liberals' struggle against despotism had been the growth of the politically active element in the various nations. By 1900, the whole or at least a large section of the adult population in most European countries could, if they wished, be politically active. Even where the process had not gone so far, as in eastern and southern Europe, the main trend was toward the development of political consciousness and the participation of an increasing number of citizens in the political affairs of the state. Political freedom meant, for the newly activated masses, a means for achieving a better life, identified with greater economic prosperity and security: where the individual failed, it was the duty of society to help him.

The socialist movement developed against this background of actual freedom, of abrupt changes, of more and more vivid consciousness of the many existing evils, of pressure exercised by growing masses of people clamoring for the intervention of society (meaning the state) in order to bring greater justice and greater happiness to everyone. During the 1830's and 1840's the terms *socialism* and *communism* had acquired a certain popularity in the industrialized countries of western Europe. Little distinction was made between the two during the period when the early socialist groups—usually consisting of a few hundred members at the utmost—were organized in France, Great Britain, and, later, Germany. This first phase of the socialist movement is known today as the phase of Utopian socialism: the term *Utopian* being used to indicate what appeared to non-socialists and to the self-styled scientific socialists of later days the impracticability of the schemes put forth by St. Simon (1760-1825), Owen (1771-1858), Fourier (1772-1837), Cabet (1776-1856), and others of that period (who inspired the foundation of various settlements in Europe and in the United States). This phase reached its climax during the revolutionary period of 1848 and came to an end with the failure of the *Commune* in France (1871).

During the fifty-odd years after St. Simon first publicized his ideas, socialism had made comparatively little headway. It had been checked mainly either by economic improvements, helped by large-scale emigration as in Great Britain, or by a show of authoritarianism, as in France under the Second Empire, or by a combination of both economic improvements and authoritarianism, as in Prussia before and under Bismarck.

By 1871 socialism had little to show. The schemes of the Utopian socialists—*phalanstères, familistères,* Owenite and Icarian colonies, national workshops—had mostly proved to be impractical. In 1847, out of the small organization Federation of the Just, whose slogan was "Proletarians of all lands unite!", had been formed the Communist League, which never had any influence and which had fizzled out by 1852. The British Christian Socialist group lasted an even shorter time. Under the leadership of Karl Marx (1818-1883), a German deeply influenced by French ideas who spent half of his life in England, and of others who prided themselves on what they called a scientific [1] approach to the study of man and man's problems, a Workingmen's Association—better known today as the First International—had been established in 1864. It represented an attempt to bring together the socialist groups which by that time had been organized in a number of European countries. They differed very widely. Some received their inspiration from the Utopian socialists of the previous generation; others from anarchistically inclined individuals like the Frenchman Proudhon (1809-1865) or the Russian Michael Bakunin (1814-1876); still others from the Italian mystic nationalist Mazzini (1805-1872) and from the German socialist nationalist Lassalle (1825-1864); in Britain, in France, in Germany, there were socialist groups of genuine Christian inspiration. Only some of the groups joined the International, in which, next to Marx, the apocalyptically minded Bakunin was the strongest personality. He advocated extreme revolutionary violence. The conflict between 'the two came to a head in 1872, and the

---

[1] Many did not find the adjective correct, *e.g.,* "The Capitalist society studied by Marx is not this or that society. . . . It is an ideal and formal society, deduced from certain hypotheses." B. Croce, *Historical Materialism and the Economics of Karl Marx* (New York: Macmillan, 1914), p. 50. "Marxism, as all utopianism . . . does not understand the relation of the eternal and unconditioned to the processes of the temporal order." R. Niebuhr in H. W. Harris, *Christianity and Communism* (Boston: Marshall Jones, 1937), p. 69.

International lingered on a few more years until it was formally dissolved in 1876.

Toward the end of the 1870's, more serious attempts were made at organizing socialist groups in European countries. In France the initiative was taken by Guesde (1845-1922) in 1877. In Great Britain, in the 1880's and early 1890's, were organized the Social Democratic Federation, which advocated changes through revolution; the Fabian Society, which advocated the same changes but through peaceful and gradual evolution (and which was joined by some of the best-known authors and statesmen of the later generation); and the Independent Labor party, linked to the trade-union movement. In Germany, William II proved to be more tolerant than Bismarck, and after the dismissal of the Iron Chancellor in 1890, restrictions imposed on the activities of socialists were lifted. After the death of Czar Alexander III (1894), a less repressive attitude on the part of the Russian government encouraged the formation, in the 1890's, of several socialist groups, among them the Social Democratic Workers' party, founded in Minsk in 1898, a successor of the small League of Struggle for the Liberation of the Working Class, founded in St. Petersburg in 1895. Similar initiatives were started in Italy, in Austria, in the Scandinavian countries, etc. All these attempts were at first feeble, limited as they were to small groups of the middle and lower classes; they were able to survive chiefly because of the freedom and tolerance that a triumphant liberalism had introduced in many European states.

By 1900 socialism had spread, but there was as yet no such thing as a unified socialist movement, in spite of the existence, since 1889, of a Second Socialist International.[2] Besides a number of minor ones, there were then seven main socialist tendencies: (1) Groups survived which took

[2] The Second International collapsed in 1914. It was revived after World War I and was active until World War II when it again disintegrated. It was replaced by a more informal organization after World War II.

their inspiration from the Utopian socialists of the first half-century, from Blanc (1811-1882), the originator of the French national workshops of 1848, from Blanqui (1805-1881) who had been a leader in socialist outbreaks in France in 1848, and 1870-1871, and from the anarchically inclined Proudhon. (2) Others, known as anarcosyndicalists, had evolved programs based on various interpretations of the doctrines of the Russian Michael Bakunin. (3) Many followed the teachings of Marx, who—more than anyone else—had produced a logical and well-integrated theory for the justification of the socialist movement and its aims. (4) In Russia, an agrarian socialism had developed which found expression first in the Populists, later in the Socialist Revolutionary party, already during the early years of the twentieth century the largest and most influential revolutionary movement in Russia. Agrarianism was appearing also in the Danubian countries and in the Balkans. (5) In Great Britain, in Germany, and elsewhere to a lesser extent, the trade-union movement (whether it called itself socialist or not) aimed more at the improvement of the workers' conditions within a capitalistic economy as an immediate objective than at the overthrow of capitalism. (6) Again in Britain first, later on the Continent, Christian socialism had made some progress. (7) In Germany had developed the theory and the practice of state socialism. Socialism in its Utopian, syndicalist, pseudo-scientific, agrarian, and laborite aspects had appeared also in the United States, but was making little headway against the powerful current of expanding democratic capitalism. The history of the years following 1900 is not only the history of the growth of socialism, but also that of the struggle between the various currents within the large stream of socialism, and of the elimination of most of them to the profit of the now existing socialist and communist parties.

Considering Europe as a whole, Marxian socialism represented by 1900 the largest and most influential section of the socialist movement. Its main tenets were:

1. the class struggle,
2. the all-determining influence of man-made social environment and the sameness of all those who live under similar economic conditions,
3. the primary role of economic or material factors,
4. the labor theory of value,
5. historical materialism (a new application of Hegelian dialectics),
6. the inevitability of capitalistic disintegration and of socialist triumph,
7. collective ownership and management of the means of production,
8. the conquest of the state for the furtherance of socialism,
9. the dictatorship of the proletariat (meaning specifically factory workers), and
10. the final obliteration of the state caused by the communization of the economy.

There were differences among Marxian socialists on such questions as the policy to be followed for the conquest of the state, some advocating violent revolutionary methods and others the use of parliamentarian institutions; on the timing of the revolution, some advocating immediacy, others maintaining, in the words of E. H. Carr, "that it was necessary to postpone . . . the revolutionary struggle of the proletariat and to concentrate meanwhile on a reformist democratic programme"; on the extent of collectivism, whether it should cover only industry, trade, and transport, or all aspects of economic activities; on the relationship between socialist organizations and the proletariat. Because of these differences, Marxian socialism was far from forming a homogeneous bloc. "A right wing, whose chief spokesman was Jean Jaurès (1852-1914), urged collaboration with other parties of the left. . . . It was . . . manifest that the workers could improve their lot within the framework of the existing societies . . . that state interference was growing and that a gradual transition from capitalism to socialism was under way." [3] A revolutionary left wing wanted to keep closer to the original teachings of Marx who "attempted to prove that the capitalist society . . . was bound to perish from inherent contradictions . . . would founder in a series of ever-increasing economic crises. The end would be the upheaval of the proletariat which was not interested in private property . . . and would organize a collectivist society instead of the existing individualistic one." [4] Between the two was the mass of the Marxian socialist movement, the so-called center, whose main spokesmen were the German K. Kautsky (1854-1938) and the Russian G. V. Plekhanov (1851-1918). It was this center, willing to use democratic procedure for the conquest of political power but opposed to collaboration with non-socialist tendencies, which controlled most of the Continental socialist parties (by 1914 an important element in those European states where there was freedom of expression and organization).

LENIN AND THE BOLSHEVIKI

Communism as we know it today owes many of its fundamental characteristics to one of its leaders and founders, whose will became law in one of the largest nations of the world. Vladimir Ilyich Ulyanov, better known as Nicolai I. Lenin (1870-1924), was born in Simbirsk, a town in what had been the independent khanate of Kazan until its conquest by Czar Ivan IV. Lenin was the son of a minor public official, descended from an impoverished noble family of mixed Slavic and Tatar origin. At an early age came the deciding crisis of his life, the hanging of his elder brother Alexander who, during the repression following the murder of Czar Alexander II (1881), had become implicated in Shelyabov's terroristic movement, "Will of the People," from which the Socialist Revolutionary party later grew.

The main points of Lenin's position and of his contribu-

[3] F. Borkenau, *World Communism* (New York: W. W. Norton, 1939), p. 19.
[4] *Ibid.*, p. 20.

tion to twentieth-century communism, can be summarized as follows:

1. From the Russian revolutionaries with whom he came in contact during his youth, Lenin absorbed the idea of violence as an indispensable means to achieve a socialist society. "The replacement of the bourgeois by the proletarian state is impossible without a violent revolution," he wrote ["Towards the Seizure of Power," in *Collected Works* (New York: International Publishers) XXI (1932), Book II, p. 166].

2. He advocated mass violence while rejecting the individual acts of terrorism in which other revolutionary groups engaged.

3. From the experiences of the Russian underground movement, Lenin derived the concept he stressed forcefully during his forty years of political activity —the necessity of creating a homogeneous group of disciplined professional revolutionaries, among whom no factionalism or dissent would be tolerated.

4. The masses were not going to lead, as most other branches of the socialist movement hoped. In considering the masses as minors, Lenin negated the validity of the fundamental liberal postulate of man's autonomy and his capacity to act on the basis of his own volition and reason.

5. Lenin accepted the Marxian theory of the "withering away" of the state in a socialist society.

6. However, instead of eliminating the state as soon as the revolution had taken place, as the anarco-syndicalists were planning, Lenin wanted to use it for the achievement of socialism. "The State control of social life, against which capitalist Liberalism so strives, is to become a reality," he stated [see *The Manifesto of the Moscow International* (Manchester: The National Labour Press, 1919), p. 5]. Also "we need the State for the transition to Socialism" ["The Revolution of 1917," in *Collected Works, op.cit.,* XX (1929), Book I, p. 140].

7. The dictatorship of the proletariat became the dictatorship of the party leading the proletariat.

8. In advocating a strong state, Lenin uncompromisingly opposed parliamentarian procedure and the liberal theory of the division of power. In his own words "the real essence of parliamentarianism is to decide every few years which member of the ruling class is to oppress the people . . . in the Commune [Soviet] a division between the legislative and executive functions no longer exists" [in *Collected Works, op.cit.,* XXI, Book II, p. 186].

9. Lenin was intolerant of any kind of compromise. When the Revolution of 1917 broke out in Russia, he directed his friends "to refuse all confidence or support to the new government" [in *Collected Works, op.cit.,* XX, Book I, p. 21].

10. Lenin saw his political party as an élite leading the proletariat into the struggle against parliamentarian democracy, capitalism, and nationalism. In the words of W. H. Chamberlin "the one-party system was Lenin's greatest contribution to modern political practice" [*Communist International* (Chicago: Human Events, 1946), p. 156].

11. Educated in the anti-nominalistic philosophy which Marx had inherited from Hegel, Lenin was concerned exclusively with groups, never with individuals; what mattered was the proletariat and not the proletarians, the bourgeoisie not the bourgeois, etc. The disregard for the individual characterizing Lenin's mentality has become one of the fundamental features of the existing communist movement—together with the corollary, Whoever belongs to an evil group must of necessity be evil.

12. An unflinching devotion to the ideal of socialism, as he called it, and a terrific capacity for work, was another important contribution Lenin made to the communist movement; for him, as for convinced communists today, everything was subordinated to the "cause."

The Social Democratic Workers' party formed by a few Russian socialists of the Marxian persuasion was, during much of its nineteen years prior to 1917, largely an underground organization, even when it had some representatives in Russia's *Duma* (Parliament). Many of its leaders lived in exile in countries of western Europe where dominant liberalism tolerated all kinds of ideas and organizations. At its second congress (in Brussels and later in London, in 1903), all the delegates agreed to accept the basic Marxian premises, thereby finally differentiating themselves from the Socialist Revolutionaries. Dissensions, however, arose between a group led by Martov (Y. O. Zederbaum, 1873-1923) and Axelrod (1850-1928), supported at times by Trotsky (L. Bronstein, 1879-1940), and a group led by Lenin, supported at that time by Plekhanov. Lenin advocated for Russia the immediate revolutionary seizure of power by the proletariat, without going through the phase of democratic liberalism, and the use of dictatorial methods to achieve the socialization of the economic system. On the question of organization Lenin, following Marx's friend F. Engels (1820-1895),[5] wanted, as Borkenau says, to sacrifice the belief in the revolutionary capacities of the proletariat to the practical necessity of forming a party of really reliable revolutionaries; while Martov and his friends, who had a Jeffersonian faith in the masses, saw in a party of professional revolutionaries a continuation of that social differentiation which they wanted to eliminate; they aimed at giving the party a wide popular basis, and wanted the members to exercise control over the leadership.

Lenin's motion, defeated by the congress (1903), was approved by a majority of the central committee of the party, and his faction was from then on known as the Bolsheviki (from *bolshintvo,* meaning majority); Martov's friends were the Mensheviki (or minority group). The two factions maintained separate organizations but remained in the same party until, at a congress in Prague in 1912, the

---

[5] It was Engels who wrote: "Conspiratorial methods . . . require a dictatorship if they are to be successful."

Bolsheviki formally established their own party. At that time it numbered in Russia, and among Russian exiles, a few thousand members only. It was numerically inferior not only to the Socialist Revolutionaries of Russia but also to the Mensheviki. It was an insignificant group compared to the millions who, outside Russia, were active members of the social democratic, syndicalist, and labor movements of western and central Europe. The strength of the Bolsheviki lay mainly in the extreme rigidity and the high degree of cohesion of their organization, and in the flexibility of their policy [6]—two elements that are among the chief characteristics of the communist organization today.

The first occasion on which the Bolsheviki could act according to their revolutionary principles came during the disorders that accompanied the Russo-Japanese war of 1904-1905. Since the financial reforms of Alexander III, industrial expansion had characterized Russian economic life, and the capital, St. Petersburg (later Petrograd, now Leningrad), had become one of the main industrial cities of the Russian Empire. Violent outbreaks against the czarist administration took place in St. Petersburg, and later in other parts of Russia. The outbreaks were the result mainly of spontaneous, unorganized movements on the part of workers and peasants. They were made possible by the relaxation of governmental coercion since the death of Alexander III, and the vacillations of his well-meaning and limited successor Nicholas II.

Socialist Revolutionaries, Mensheviki and Bolsheviki alike, were quick to seize the occasion. In order to give organization and direction to popular rioting, they formed revolutionary committees called Soviets, which purported to be the expression of the will of the toiling masses and to be composed of representatives of workers and peasants.

[6] The Bolsheviki "reorganized as an ultra-centralized party, under military discipline [were] not a democratic self-governing party open to all, but rather like a medieval order of knightly monks." V. Chernov, *The Great Russian Revolution* (New Haven: Yale University Press, 1936), p. 431.

The most important one, that determined later the manner in which other Soviets were organized, was the St. Petersburg Soviet. Its first president was a Menshevik; after his arrest he was replaced by Trotsky who, although a member of the Social Democratic party, had tried to keep out of the quarrel between Mensheviki and Bolsheviki. It was at that time that Lenin met his future successor, Joseph Stalin (Joseph Vissarionovitch Djugasvilli) (1879-   ). The 1905 Soviets had played only a minor role in the general revolutionary attempts of that period. But they had struck the imagination of revolutionary Russians, and as time passed more and more importance was attributed to them. The Soviets came to represent the spirit and the essence of revolutionism, and from then on the term became, for the Bolsheviki as well as for the others, synonymous both with violent socialist revolution and with the political structure created by the Revolution. To the Parliament, in which all sections of the population should be represented, the Bolsheviki opposed the Soviet, an assembly in which only the working masses were represented.

World War I deepened the cleavage between the various socialist groups of Europe, particularly the Marxists who—in relation to the war—found themselves split into three main factions: those who supported the war effort of their national governments (social patriots); those who opposed the war effort and were for peace immediately at any cost (pacifists); and those who were against the war effort of their governments but did not want peace, their aim being the transformation of what they called an imperialistic war into civil wars against bourgeois and autocratic governments (revolutionaries).

To the first group belonged, in the beginning, the majority of German socialists, at that time the largest and most influential socialistic group in Europe, and a majority of the Belgian and French socialists (Guesde joined the French Cabinet) and of the British Labor party. Most Scandinavian socialists were willing to support the war effort of the Allies. In Russia, Plekhanov was for cooperation with the czarist government, and, at least at the beginning, also Kamenev (L. B. Rosenfeld, 1883-1936, Trotsky's brother-in-law), and, according to some sources, Stalin. Among the pacifists were the majority of socialists in the Austrian Empire, in Italy, and in the Balkans; many moderate German socialists under Bernstein (1850-1932); the British socialists who followed MacDonald (1866-1937); and most Mensheviki under Martov and Axelrod, then actively supported by Trotsky. Opposed to both the social patriots and the pacifists, and forming the smallest of the three groups, were Lenin [7] and the Bolsheviki; the followers of K. Radek (1885-?), and the Spartakus Bund led by K. Liebknecht (1871-1919) and R. Luxemburg (1870-1919) in Germany; the International Socialist Women's Movement led by Clara Zetkin; the International Socialist Youth Organization led by W. Munzenberg; small groups in Holland and in Sweden; and the majority of the anarco-syndicalists.

The pre-war cleavage between right, center, and left had not upset the unity of the Marxian socialist movement to the extent that World War I did. Representatives of the pacifist tendency met at Zimmerwald, Switzerland, in 1915 in an attempt to use the influence of the socialist parties to end the war. They organized themselves into a group, with Balabanova as secretary, which was supported by Bernstein, MacDonald, the Swede Branting (1860-1925), the Italian socialists, etc. If one considers that most social patriots were ideological pacifists and had accepted the war only as an evil necessity, it was natural that the influence of the pacifists should increase. Already in 1917 many French socialists were protesting against the continuation of the war, and in 1918 the majority of socialists in the German *Reichstag* joined hands with members of the Catholic and democratic parties in voting against further credits for the war.

---

[7] "Our main task is to guard against . . . unity with the social patriots or . . . with the wavering ones like Trotsky and Co." Lenin, "The Revolution of 1917," in *Collected Works* (New York: International Publishers, 1929), XX, Book I, p. 21.

Representatives of the revolutionaries had attended the meeting at Zimmerwald and had agreed with the pacifists in condemning the "imperialistic" war. But they refused to condemn war as an instrument of social change and met in 1916, at Kienthal, also in Switzerland, to elaborate their own program. The break between the revolutionary left and the rest of the socialist movement was more than a question of program: it was the manifestation of two opposing temperaments, the tolerant humanitarianism represented by the pacifists and the violent intolerance of the leftist revolutionaries. The war helped to crystallize the difference between moderate socialism, then forming the majority of the European socialist movement, and extreme socialism, which later became the communist movement. Moderate socialism opposed liberalism, but it had absorbed to a considerable extent the liberal spirit and was willing to operate within the framework of democratic institutions. Extreme socialism rejected the ideas, the spirit, and the institutions of liberalism.

THE COMMUNIST REVOLUTION IN RUSSIA

It may or may not be correct that "the corrupt reactionaries in control of the Czar's Court deliberately undertook to wreck Russia in order to make a separate peace with Germany." [8] But there is little doubt that influential circles within the Russian government, leading probably to the Czarina and her favorites, wanted at all costs to get Russia out of World War I. The strikes of March 1917 [9] could have been repressed more severely if there had not been officials in high places who wanted to prove to the Allies that Russia could not carry on with the war.

Since 1889, May 1 (Labor Day) had been the socialist

[8] J. Reed, *Ten Days That Shook the World* (New York: International Publishers, 1926), p. viii.

[9] February, according to the Julian calendar then in force; March, according to the Western calendar which was adopted at the beginning of 1918.

symbol of the workers' struggle against capitalism. For many years Russian industrial workers had struck on that day and, as usual, preparation began some time ahead with strikes here and there. Moreover, economic conditions were deteriorating rapidly. Among the large working population of Petrograd there was acute consciousness of the need for better wages, for food, and, more than anything, for peace. The war had already lasted over two and a half years, and casualties had been appalling. How the strikes got out of hand and the czarist regime collapsed cannot be discussed here, and has probably not yet been evaluated correctly by any historian. When the collapse took place, there were several groups willing to fill the political vacuum left by the disintegration of the Czar's authority. Numerically the most important was the group of Socialist Revolutionaries, the Russian version of the agrarian socialist movement. Their socialism was economically of the cooperativistic variety, and politically of the federalistic. They rejected both the theory and the practice of state omnipotence. According to Chernov, one of their leaders, the Socialist Revolutionaries "realized that Russia's toiling masses lacked . . . maturity, and . . . training; . . . they visualized [between capitalism and socialism] a long transition period of 'laborism' . . . the building of a new social legislation within the framework of a money economy." They were divided between a right-wing majority and a left-wing minority. To the right of the Socialist Revolutionaries was the small group of Trudoviki or Laborites. Among their leaders had been a young lawyer and deputy to the *Duma,* A. Kerenski (1881-   ), who later joined the Socialist Revolutionary party. The two other socialist groups were the Marxian Mensheviki and Bolsheviki. The Kadets (Democrats) and the Octobrists (so called because they had supported the constitution granted by the czar in October 1905) represented Western liberalism and constitutional monarchy, respectively. Both Kadets and Octobrists were more influential in the *Duma* (elected on the basis of limited suffrage) than among the people; they derived their support from the majority of the Russian middle class and from the enlightened minority of the upper classes—two groups which included only a small fraction of the Russian nation. There were—particularly among the officers of the armed forces, the landowners, and other privileged groups—many supporters of the czarist autocracy, but it took them nearly a year to recover from the confusion into which they were thrown by the revolution of March 1917.

In the capital, the various groups struggled for power in the provisional government, in the *Duma,* in the newly established Soviet, in a multiplicity of committees, clubs, and leagues which had mushroomed overnight. In the streets and the squares there were parades, meetings, and demonstrations—and some violence (remarkably little at first). Many so-called "leaders" had little or no organized following; they made speeches and wrote articles, while paying little attention to the necessity of building up a cohesive following, and forgetting that organized force is a fundamental instrument of political action. "While Kerenski [then Prime Minister] was measuring the floors of the Winter Palace in solitude, the Military Revolutionary Committee was taking action on a vast scale," Trotsky was to write later, comparing his own activity with the inaction of Kerenski at the time of the October revolution.

During the months immediately following the March revolution, what happened in the provinces was of greater importance than what happened in the capital. For the masses of Russian peasants, the abdication of the Czar meant that there was no longer a government, that it was possible to realize the aspiration of most peasants in most countries at most times: to own the soil. As in France shortly after the meeting of the Estates General in 1789, so there was in Russia, soon after the March revolution, a *jacquerie,* the unorganized and all-powerful revolt of the tillers of the soil. It is usually difficult to get the peasantry to move; once they start, it is even more difficult to stop them; where they form a large percentage of the population (as was the case in Russia in 1917) they can crush everything under their weight. The peasants began to kill the landlords and to divide the soil among themselves; the soldiers (most of whom were peasants) began to kill their officers (most of whom were landlords); the workers in the the towns and the miners (most of whom were only a few years removed from the soil) began to kill their employers. As time went on the movement acquired impetus; in many parts of Russia authority collapsed and the administration disintegrated. The riots in the capital had led to the abdication of the Czar; the *jacquerie* destroyed the organization of the Russian state; it was the real revolution, and it created the chaos which a few months later was to enable a small but determined minority to establish itself as the new Russian state.

The war against Germany was a complicating factor. In the name of the democracy in which they believed, Kadets, Mensheviki, and the majority of the Socialist Revolutionaries were for the continuation of the war. The Bolsheviki, following the line set by Lenin at Zimmerwald and at Kienthal, opposed the continuation of the war on the side of the Allies. This attitude seemed to justify those who thought that the Bolsheviki were nothing but German agents; they proved, however, to be better representatives of the aspirations of the dynamic sections of the masses.

At the time, the Bolsheviki were not numerous. Lenin is reported by Chernov, a Socialist Revolutionary leader, to have estimated the total number of Bolsheviki in the whole of Russia at about 240,000 in July 1917, of whom 32,000 were in Petrograd. An American expert on Russian and communist affairs, F. L. Schuman, states that "the army of the faithful numbered only 40,000 in April 1917, and only 115,000 early in 1918." Another expert, E. H. Carr, accepts the doctored official history of the Russian Communist party and gives the figure of 23,600 for February 17, 1917—it is difficult to see how, under the conditions then existing in Russia, the party administration could keep such an exact count of the membership. Other authorities give figures varying from a minimum of not more than 10,000 Bolsheviki, at the outbreak of the revolution, to around 100,000 by the time they seized power. Whatever the exact total, the Bolsheviki in 1917 were numerically a rather insignificant group, drawn from the intellectuals [10] rather than from the workers. When rioting in Russia's capital acquired the aspect of a revolt, the Bolsheviki at first were uncertain about what attitude to take. Several leaders apparently played with the idea of abandoning the intransigence characteristic of the party and collaborating with other anti-czarist groups. The arrival of Lenin at the beginning of April on the "sealed wagon" which the German authorities had put at the disposal of several Russian exiles and which brought them from Switzerland to Russia, put an end to the vacillations of the Bolsheviki, who now were joined by Trotsky and his friends (about 4,000 of them).

As the result of the March revolution, two conflicting authorities existed in Petrograd: the provisional government, first under Prince Lvov (1861-1925), later under Kerenski, supported by a coalition of political groups represented in the *Duma,* and the Soviet, organized chiefly by Socialist Revolutionaries and Mensheviki, under the leadership of the moderate socialist Chkheidze, and supposed to represent the will of the workers, peasants, and soldiers. The same dualism existed in the provinces. The Bolsheviki wanted to have nothing in common with the provisional government. "The new government cannot bring peace . . . cannot give the people bread . . . nor full freedom," wrote Lenin. And Trotsky echoed: "The

[10] According to Carr, *The Bolshevik Revolution, 1917-1923* (New York: Macmillan, 1951), p. 207, even later, on the eve of the party purges of 1921-1922, the intellectuals represented more than half the total membership. This would seem to support the opinion of those who maintain that communism is not so much a "proletarian" movement as an expression of extreme dissatisfaction among the intellectual section of the middle classes.

handing over of power to the Liberals . . . will become
. . . a source of headlessness of the revolution, enormous
chaos, embitterment of the masses, collapse of the front,
and in the future extreme bitterness of the civil war." To
avoid the encumbrances and limitations of parliamentary
procedure "the Soviet of Workers', Soldiers' and Peasants'
deputies must at once take every practical and feasible step
for the realization of socialism" [Lenin, *op.cit.*, XX, Book I,
p. 159]; that meant replacing the Socialist Revolutionaries
and the Mensheviki in the Soviets with Bolsheviki. Lenin
recognized that "the majority of the deputies were on the
side of the parties of the Social Democratic Mensheviki
and Socialist Revolutionaries" [Lenin, *op.cit.*, XXI, Book
I, p. 84]. What was meant by Soviet government was explained by Trotsky: "In the system of Soviet dictatorship
not even a secondary place was found for democratic repre-
sentation" when the Bolsheviki took over. Mensheviki and
Socialist Revolutionaries were weakened by internal conflicts and by the attempt to act according to theoretical
schemes which had little relation to the reality of a population desiring only peace and a share in the wealth of the
rich. More important than the influence of the Soviets was
the organization, in October, of an armed force, the work of
Trotsky who headed a Military Revolutionary Committee
controlling several thousand enthusiastic proletarians.

On October 24, 1917 (old calendar), the second congress of Soviets met in Petrograd. During the night the
military squads organized by Trotsky occupied the key
points of the capital. Kerenski fled. The Bolsheviki formed
a new government under Lenin, whose slogan "Bread, Peace,
and Freedom" had attracted larger and larger groups of
the population. The success of the Bolsheviki seems hardly
credible: it can be explained only by taking into account
their cohesion, the decisiveness of their leaders, the ruthless use of violence, the disintegration of the Russian state,
the divisions and armed weakness of their opponents, the
pressure of foreign (German) attack, and the will to peace
of the Russian nation.

The next few months witnessed the firm decision of the Bolshevik government to remain in power, whatever the internal and external opposition. The elections for the Constituent Assembly, decided upon by the *Duma* and the provisional government, took place under conditions of considerable, even if relative, freedom. The Bolsheviki, who had received about one fourth of the votes, had 175 deputies [11] elected against 410 for the Socialist Revolutionaries, who had received over two thirds of the votes; the Mensheviki (16 deputies), Kadets (17 deputies), and other groups were also represented. The Constituent Assembly met on January 5 (old calendar), after the Kadets had been outlawed and a number of Socialist Revolutionary leaders had been arrested. In spite of these intimidations the Assembly voted a motion of no-confidence in the Bolshevik government. The latter reacted by repeating that the Constituent Assembly no longer represented the will of the people, and ordering its dissolution, which was carried out that night by the troops organized by Trotsky. This was the end of Russia's democratic experiment. In March 1918, at the seventh party congress, the official name of the Bolshevik faction was changed to *Communist party,* to emphasize the difference between the Bolsheviki and the rest of the socialist movement.

During the first eight months of the Bolshevik regime little was done to introduce collectivism in the country. Lenin, who knew what to destroy but had only a vague idea of how to organize the collectivist society, considered this a transitional period during which a mixed economy would exist, partly state-managed and partly private. The plan was, apparently, to transform Russia gradually from an agrarian to a modern industrial nation, to extend the sphere of nationalized enterprises in industry and trade, while at the same time taxation and controls would check the growth of a new economic middle class. By the end of May 1918 (new calendar), only 300 concerns and some agricultural

[11] Figures vary. Those quoted here are from Carr, *op. cit.,* p. 110.

estates representing about 4 percent of the tilled land of the country had been nationalized.

The decision to put an end to the first brief "transitional" period and to attempt the over-all introduction of collectivism was taken as a result of the political disintegration of Russia, which grew after the *coup d'état* of October 1917. At the end of 1918 the communist government exercised authority over areas inhabited by less than one fourth of the Russian population. The war with Germany had come to an end in March 1918; but the Germans were in control of most of the Ukraine, of the Baltic provinces, White Russia, and the Crimea. An anti-Bolshevik force in Finland had defeated the Bolsheviki. There was an independent Menshevik government in Georgia. Socialist Revolutionaries had organized their own separate governments in western Siberia and in parts of the valley of the Volga. Groups of the former imperial army were in control of various provinces. Opposition to the Bolshevik government was increasing in the areas of central Russia, where its control was greatest; the opposition there was led mostly by Socialist Revolutionaries. Cooperation was being established between different groups of the opposition. In this way there came into existence the democratic League for the Regeneration of Russia which, according to Shub's biography of Lenin, "looked to the aid of England, France and the United States, and made an official request to those countries to restore an Allied front in Russia,"—reactionary groups organized the Right Center, which asked for German support; middle-of-the-road elements formed the National Center; a people's army was organized in the eastern districts of European Russia by members of the Constituent Assembly.

The Bolsheviki (now communists) had seized power by force. Eight months later it was evident that the limited popular support they had enjoyed was waning, and that only through force could they keep themselves in power. Stalin had declared that the Bolsheviki were opposed to the restoration of the police force, and Lenin had apparently dreamed that the Russians would willingly fall in with the communists. The choice now was between terror and failure. Under the guidance of Dzerzhinsky (entrusted a few months earlier with the formation of a special political police, the *Cheka*), a reign of terror was established to eliminate all opposition in the areas still controlled by the communist government. Anti-communist revolutionaries (anarchists, Socialist Revolutionaries, and Mensheviki) were liquidated as savagely as the liberals (Kadets and Octobrists), and the members of the former privileged groups. Out of the remnants of the Russian armies, of party members, and refugees from the regions which no longer recognized the authority of the central government, a Red army was organized by Trotsky, whose energy was probably the most important single factor in saving communism at the most crucial period of its development.

In the economic field an attempt was made to bring all available resources under the control of the government for the strengthening of its authority and the supplying of the Red army. All industrial concerns were now nationalized; the peasants were compelled to surrender the major part of their produce to the government; private ownership of homes was abolished, as was money, which was replaced with a system of coupons.

The struggle for the elimination of organized opposition against the communist regime lasted nearly three years, or a little longer if one takes into account events on the periphery of the Russian state. The Menshevik regime in Georgia was defeated in February 1921, the pan-Turanian leader Enver Pasha was killed and his followers dispersed in August 1922, and the Far Eastern Republic sponsored originally by the Japanese was re-incorporated in the Russian state in November 1922. After the liquidation of the Socialist Revolutionaries (facilitated by their internal divisions), the greatest threat to the communist regime was represented by the "White" armies organized in the Arctic north, in the Baltic areas, in the south, in Siberia—to which can be added the troops of the newly established Polish republic which attacked Russia in 1920. The description of the happenings of those years belongs properly to the history of Russia. For our purposes, it is enough to mention that jealousies between leaders, excesses which alienated the peasant population, the aggressiveness, determination, and courage of the Red army, and Trotsky's genius and ruthlessness put to an end the "White" opposition after two and a half years of furious and bloody fighting. A limited amount of help had been given by some Allied powers to some of the anti-communist forces: not enough to win,[12] but enough to provide a further rationalization for the intense hatred of the communists toward anything Western. Intervention began with Japanese landings in the Maritime Province in April 1918; the Allies followed a few months later. At the peak of their strength, foreign forces numbered about 100,000 men: of these, nearly 70,000 were Japanese in the Siberian Far East; the few thousand Americans, sent to the same area, had the mission of checking the Japanese rather than of fighting the communists. The rest of the foreign troops (British, French, Czechs) were spread from Siberia to Odessa on the Black Sea, from Arkhangelsk to Tiflis in Georgia—not a force but a farce.

The end of the civil war found Russia exhausted. In spite of the victory, dissatisfaction, as exemplified by the Kronstadt revolt (March 1921) at the cry of "the Soviets without the Communists" was widespread. Terror had all but destroyed the will to opposition among the educated

[12] The Allied governments were often undecided on the question of help to the "White" armies. Lord Curzon, on August 16, 1919, remarked in a draft memorandum: "The situation is so complex and the difficulties of arriving at decision . . . are so great that . . . it would be no exaggeration to admit that there is no policy at all." G. Stewart, *The White Armies of Russia* (New York: Macmillan, 1933), p. 286. Finally (in 1920), the Allies flatly refused to help the "White" armies: "Great Britain urged that . . . if he [Wrangel] . . . should attack the Bolsheviks, His Majesty's government would be unable to concern itself further with the fate of his army." *Ibid.*, p. 370.

classes; but it was doubtful whether it would have the same effect on the uneducated masses, which were becoming more and more restive, and whether it would be enough to keep the government in power. To satisfy large sections of the population, both in the rural areas and in the cities, the tenth party congress (March 1921) decided to recognize private trade and small-scale private production, thereby introducing the New Economic Policy (NEP) which represented a return to Lenin's transitional period in the early stages of the regime. Violent disputes arose at once between Trotsky, Bukharin (1888-1938), Kamenev, Tomsky (1880-1936), Rykov (1881-1938), and others, over the extent of the concessions to be made to non-socialist economic forces, with Lenin acting as final arbiter.

The success of the Bolshevik revolution in Russia was of fundamental importance in the later development of the communist movement. If communism had remained confined to the West, it would probably have died out like anarchism, syndicalism, and other extreme movements brought into existence by the freeing of human energies; in the West the democratic trend was strong enough to eliminate movements it could not absorb. Their success in Russia gave to the communists the backing of one of the most powerful states in the world. Moreover, the triumph in Russia strengthened those traits in the communist movement that are closely linked to a culture which has hardly known—and cares less—for the elements that made possible the development of modern free Western societies: respect for the dignity of the individual, moderation, belief in the superiority of government by discussion and of the rule of law, and legitimacy of opposition and dissent. Socialism had been a development of Western civilization; it had derived its strength from a deep humanitarian impulse; it might have been mistaken in the assumption that collectivism produces greater liberty than capitalism, but it was animated by a sincere desire to achieve greater individual liberty. Communism was socialism interpreted by a society characterized to the highest degree by political autocracy and intellectual intolerance; it was unlimited collectivism, to be realized through the integral collectivization not only of the economy but of all forms of human activities.

THE REVOLUTIONARY PHASE OF THE COMINTERN (1918-1923)

At the time of the armistices which put an end to World War I (September-November 1918), conditions seemed to favor the success of revolutionary movements in many parts of Europe. Human suffering had been great; the war had affected practically every family in most of the countries; the institutions established during the nineteenth century had weakened; economic losses had been heavy; four years of deep nervous tension were bound to cause a reaction. Besides the Russian Empire, the German, Austro-Hungarian, and Turkish Empires had collapsed. These, together with the Balkan states overrun by the contending armies, covered two thirds of the European continent. Confusion and chaos reigned over large areas. Elsewhere, there was considerable tension. In Italy, in France, even in the British Isles, many worried about the possibility of a social revolution. Here was an ideal situation for small groups to seize the political initiative. The Russian revolution had caused repercussions in every corner of the Continent. It had raised the hopes of the revolutionaries; its excesses [13] had terrified moderates and conservatives alike.

Immediately after the ending of hostilities, the small socialist groups in various countries which shared the ideology of the Bolsheviki made a definite attempt to follow Lenin's example and to seize power. The attempts failed. In Finland, the revolutionary government set up by Kuusinen, leader of the leftists among the Social Democrats, had

[13] "The butcher's bill, from Soviet sources . . . totalled 1,572,718, . . . [and] the famine cost the lives of four to six million peasants." W. R. Inge, in H. Wilson Harris, *Christianity and Communism* (Boston: Marshall Jones, 1937), p. 41.

been defeated through the combined effort of anti-communist Finns and German troops. In the former Baltic provinces (which had become the independent republics of Lithuania, Latvia, and Estonia) the presence of Germans and of "White" (anti-revolutionary) Russians made the organization of a communist movement impossible. In Poland, the nationalistically minded Socialist party led by Pilsudski (1867-1935) won over the more extremist Social Democratic party. Rumanians were more interested in wresting Transylvania from Hungary and Bessarabia from Russia than in revolutions. In Bulgaria the peasants' Agrarian party led by Stamboliiski (1879-1923), in power since September 1918, was close to the Bolsheviki's bitter foes, the Socialist Revolutionaries. In Hungary, moderate republicans led by Karolyi were able to form a government, and in Austria the powerful left-inclined socialists under Otto Bauer (1881-1938), besides being opposed to the violent means used by the communists in Russia and advocated elsewhere by communist sympathizers, were convinced that the time was not ripe for socialism. In Czechoslovakia, nationalism and liberalism won over revolutionary socialism.

It was in Germany that conditions appeared to be most favorable for the development of a situation similar to that in Russia. It was there that existed what had been for years the strongest, largest, and best-organized socialist movement in Europe. Majority Socialists and Independent Socialists (the social patriots and the pacifists hated by Lenin and his friends) had the support of the majority of German industrial workers and of large sections of the middle classes. But the more radical socialist groups, the Spartacists and the Shop Stewards, also had a considerable following. This proved, however, to be inadequate. In November 1918 Majority and Independent Socialists had formed a provisional government which repressed without difficulty the sporadic risings organized in December by the extremists. Through the initiative of Rosa Luxemburg and Karl Liebknecht, a Communist party (the first outside Russia) was formed on December 31, 1918. It organized a new and more important rising for the middle of January 1919. This failed, and the two leaders were killed. In Berlin, as in Petrograd, a Workers' and Soldiers' Council (Soviet) had been organized; but instead of trying to overthrow the provisional government, in the words of Borkenau it "voted itself out of power by a big majority, deciding to hold the polls for a Constituent Assembly," loyally respecting the expression of the popular will. In southern Germany the revolutionary movement had apparently petered out with the formation in Bavaria of a provisional government under the pacifist socialist Kurt Eisner (1867-1919), a foe of the communists.

It was evident that the revolution would not take place as easily as had been hoped. The Bolshevik leaders called a conference in Moscow (now the capital of Russia) in order to launch an international organization through which the revolutionary groups following the line of the Russian communists could help each other. It was maintained that by strengthening the revolutionary groups in the countries of western and central Europe, a general European revolution could follow in the wake of the Russian one. The meeting was not well attended. On March 7, 1919, the Communist International was launched—the *Comintern,* as it came to be known all over the world. The first secretary was Angelica Balabanova, a pacifist. Lenin's friend Gregori Zinovief was appointed president; among his collaborators were Bukharin and Radek. "Lenin," says Borkenau, "stood for an international which should begin as a small body and be under the strictest control of his party. . . . [He] reacted against the catastrophe of western revolutionary Marxism by attempting to introduce the principle of the Russian professional revolutionary organization into the western movement." Hopes were high. Zinovief prophesied that "within a year . . . all Europe would be a Soviet Republic." Great effort was made to realize the hopes: the four and a half years from March 1919 to October 1923 saw a series of definite attempts on the Comintern's part to achieve a communist dictatorship in several European countries.

The murder of Kurt Eisner in Munich induced the local Independent Socialists to proclaim a Soviet republic on April 7, 1919. Six days later this government was overthrown by the communists under the leadership of Eugene Leviné. Unable to organize the defense of the city, attacked by the troops of the predominantly Social Democratic central government, the communist regime was ousted by the other socialist groups under the leadership of the poet Ernst Toller. On May 1 the government troops entered Munich, and Leviné was killed.

In Hungary the provisional government under Karolyi resigned on March 20, 1919, as a protest against excessive Allied demands. With the help of the socialists, the communist Béla Kun (1886-?) set up a new regime which included, as commissar of commerce, Mathias Rakosi (who after the events of 1944-1947 became the real ruler of Hungary). The new government immediately abolished private property in all means of production and decreed the death penalty for everyone engaging in trade. The Russians, pressed by several "White" offensives, were unable to send any help; Rumanians and "White" Hungarians attacked the new Soviet republic; the excesses committed by Tibor Szamuely, a firm believer in the most ruthless violence, alienated the masses, particularly in western Hungary; the Austrian socialists refused to help the Hungarian extremists. The Hungarian Soviet republic collapsed on August 19, 1919, and was replaced by a government of moderate trade-unionists, soon overthrown by reactionary groups. Europeans at the time were shocked by the excesses of Béla Kun's regime, which strengthened anti-communist feeling, and magnified the fear on which reactionary movements thrive.

During this period the cleavage between democratically minded socialists and the communists increased. The tension between the former social patriots and the pacifists prevented the reconstruction of the Second International at the two meetings of March 1919 in Bern and of August of the same year in Lucerne, but there was no doubt that the two wings were closer to each other than to the communist groups. Former anti-war socialists, including among others the Independent Socialists of Germany and the French and Austrian Socialist parties (the so-called Reconstructionists), launched in 1921 a new International (the Second-and-a-half International), supported by the Trade-Union International organized in Amsterdam by Edo Fimmen.

This development was interpreted as an act of hostility against the communists and induced the leaders of the Comintern to adopt a more intransigent attitude, exemplified in the communication they sent to the Independent Socialists of Germany. In this communication they criticized "the idea that the support of the majority of the people is necessary for the establishment of the proletarian dictatorship; [the] rejection of revolutionary terrorism; lack of readiness to face civil war; lack of understanding of the necessity of wrecking the machinery of the bourgeois state; [the] petty-bourgeois insistence upon the safe-guarding of democratic liberties; [the] useless attempts to win the lower middle classes; [the] vague talk about nationalization, when a clear-cut fight for expropriation without compensation would be necessary."

To strengthen the communist movement, the second world congress of the Third (Communist) International had been held in July 1920. It was attended by delegates of the Russian Communist party, the Italian, Norwegian and Bulgarian Socialist parties, the Czech Left Socialists, the Communist parties of Hungary and Austria, both the German Communist party and the German Independent Socialist party, etc. It approved a twenty-one-point program which stressed the decision to fight not only the "bourgeoisie" but also all reformist, reconstructionist, centrist, patriot, and anti-war socialists; it required the development of underground organizations; the infiltration of the armies of the various countries; the winning over of the peasantry; the breaking of the Trade-Union International; the obedience of communist parliamentarian groups wherever they existed to the executive committees of the various parties; the centralization of authority in all communist parties, and their subordination to the Comintern; periodical purges, and the exclusion of all members who did not vote for affiliation with the Communist International.

Attempts were made to bring together the various factions, but they failed before the intransigence of both communists and social democrats, deeply divided on the fundamental problems of human freedom, individual rights, and the use of violence. When the Second-and-a-half International of former anti-war socialists tried to bring together the Third International (the Comintern) and the Second International finally reconstructed by the social democratic factions, the Belgian socialist Vandervelde asked, as price for the agreement, that Russia adopt representative institutions, freedom of press and propaganda for the non-communist socialist groups of Russia, the liberation of Russian Socialist Revolutionary leaders, and the recognition of the independence of Georgia. These requests were refused by Lenin and Zinovief (except that the Socialist Revolutionaries were not sentenced to death); thus the projected unification of the many branches of the socialist movement failed, the field being clearly divided between democrats (the Second International) and anti-democrats (the Third International), between socialists whose collectivistic aspirations were checked by the European liberal tradition, and integral or totalitarian socialists. Nineteenth-century socialism had been anti-liberal because it wanted more liberalism; it had operated on the basis of two contradictory elements (liberal aspirations and hatred for liberalism) which now were clearly divorced. Social democrats came to the conclusion that the desired extension of liberalism was incompatible with the destruction of what liberalism had achieved (democracy); communists denied liberalism *in toto*.

Having achieved greater cohesion within their own movement, the communist leaders renewed their revolutionary efforts. But now the tide was against them. A few small risings, like the one in Estonia, failed even to arouse popular interest. In Italy there was practically a state of civil war in 1921 and 1922, but the communists made little or no headway. The last serious attempt of the communists during this phase took place in Germany in October 1923, when Brandler, then the leader of the German Communist party, was ordered to prepare for a rising. He accepted first a post in the coalition cabinet of the state of Saxony, with the aim of acquiring control over the police. The rising took place, but the population remained indifferent, and the troops of the central government had no difficulty in suppressing the revolt. The Communist party was outlawed in Germany but was allowed to revive a few months later.

Although Europe was, and remained for a considerable time, the main theater of communist activities, attempts were made during this first phase of the Comintern to develop communist organization elsewhere. The United States, before World War I, had witnessed the expansion of some socialistic movements; among them the Socialist party, which had increased its voting strength ninefold between 1900 and 1912, and the I.W.W., basically a syndicalist organization. The syndicalists, among whom at the time was W. Z. Foster, later secretary of the American Communist party, emphasized the use of force and violent revolution, and had decided to transfer the functions of the state to the hands of workers' organizations as soon as they were able to gain power. The great majority of the socialists accepted instead the free political institutions and the fundamental ideological principles of the American republic. A minority, although disagreeing with the syndicalists on the position of the state, were convinced that violence was required to bring about a social revolution; [14] these constituted the so-called "left wing," whose members sympathized warmly with the Russian Bolsheviki. Factional strife was intense.

[14] Concerning the role of violence, American communists were not different from other communists: "Some form of violence is unavoidable." E. Browder, *What Is Communism?* (New York: Vanguard Press, 1936), p. 169.

In 1919, from the left wing of the Socialist party, arose a Communist party and a Communist Labor party. They represented a negligible element in the life of the American nation,[15] being based on unassimilated groups, whose communism was often nothing but an expression of Slavic nationalism, and on the unstable fringe of the intelligentsia.

The repression at the end of 1919, caused chiefly by the reaction against the excesses of communism in Europe, drove the communists underground. In 1920 an effort was made to unite the Communist party and the Communist Labor party, which combined to form the United Communist party. Under the conditions of freedom and personal security enjoyed by American citizens communist leaders found it impossible to enforce unity among the few thousand communists then existing in the country, and by the end of 1921 there were no less than twelve different communist organizations, each group accusing the other of being "petty bourgeois," an accusation which implied attachment to the institutions of liberal democracy and unwillingness to use collective terrorism. The economic crisis of 1921 seemed to provide a favorable juncture for a revolutionary movement. Several warring communist factions joined hands in the Workers' party. To help in the unification, Moscow sent a representative, who ordered rebellious members to join the Workers' party. Following the directives of the Comintern, the American communists devoted themselves to the formation of a cohesive communist organization and to the development of "fronts" through which a large number of people could be reached.

In China, where political disintegration had increased rapidly after the revolution of 1911, a Communist party had been established in 1921. As the result of an agreement between Sun Yat-sen (1866-1925), leader of a vaguely

---

[15] "At its very inception in 1919 the [communist] movement never had over 35,000 or 40,000 members. . . . All but a thousand of the organized communists were of immigrant origin. . . . By 1927 . . . [it] had less than 8,000 members." J. Oneal and G. A. Werner, *American Communism* (New York: Dutton, 1947), p. 11.

democratic section of the revolutionary movement, and the Soviet rulers in 1923, the Chinese communists, under the guidance of the Soviet representative Borodin, made a definite effort to conquer Sun's party, the Kuomintang,[16] which became a model of the Russian Communist party. There was a semblance of democratic control by the members and a reality of domination by a small group. But many feared that success for the revolution at the price of communist leadership would mean that it was a Russian, not a Chinese, revolution. As a result, after the death of Sun Yat-sen, a struggle broke out between the strictly nationalistic wing of the Kuomintang, led by Chiang Kai-shek (1887-   ), and the communists, which led to the departure of the Russian agents and, at least for a while, to the unification of most of China under nationalist leadership. Pockets of communist activity remained here and there under various leaders, among whom the ablest and most energetic was Mao Tse-tung (1893-   ), son of a central China peasant.

By 1923, with the exception of China, non-Russian communism was definitely on the defensive. Revolutionary activity had not led to the hoped-for results. Agrarianism (in Bulgaria), nationalism (in Poland and Rumania), fascism (in Italy and in Hungary), social democracy (in Germany, Austria, and Scandinavia), and liberalism (in France, the smaller western European democracies, and the English-speaking world) had proved to be stronger than communism. The communist leaders recognized the situation for what it was and acted accordingly. For several years they devoted their entire energies to the consolidation of the movement and not to revolutionary activities, in order to be ready when another opportunity for revolution should arise.

[16] "Mao Tse-tung . . . was said to be in Chiang Kai-shek's counsels until Chiang Kai-shek brought the revolution to an end in 1927." R. Payne, *The Revolt of Asia* (New York: Day, 1947), p. 143.

2

From 1923 to the End of World War II

INTERNAL CONFLICTS, RETREAT, AND CONSOLIDATION (1923-1934)

THE period 1923-1934 was devoted mostly to organization and propaganda, and witnessed the introduction of the first Five Year Plan in Russia. An effort was made to give all communist movements those characteristics of internal discipline, centralized direction, and intolerance of any kind of opposition or deviation which Lenin had infused in the Russian Bolsheviki. This period also saw the ideological foundation of Stalinism, supposedly a revised form of communism. The death of Lenin (January 21, 1924), previously incapacitated for several months, increased the tension between various communist factions in and outside Russia. For some the conflict was an ideological one, for others a sordid competition for power. Probably both elements existed. Ideologically, it is difficult at times to see exactly where each of the main protagonists stood. But the situation cleared as more and more power was centered in the hands of Stalin, the general secretary of the Communist party of the Soviet Union, while his opponents were thrown together. There were dissents between Stalin, Trotsky, and others on internal and external questions, on the NEP, the policy toward the peasants, the attitude to be adopted toward other socialist or non-socialist movements, immediate revolution or a cautious long-range policy. Trotsky, who according to many admirers had "laid the foundation of what had arisen in Russia" and who had declared "we will deal with the enemies of the revolution and its saboteurs with an iron hand," saw the iron hand being applied to himself. The split between him and Stalin on the main issues of world revolution *versus* socialism in Russia, which had been apparent since 1921, led in 1925 to the isolation of Trotsky, unable to stand the aggressiveness and able maneuvering of Stalin, the party boss. In 1927, when officials who owed their jobs to Stalin had chosen all the delegates to the fifteenth party congress, Trotsky, Zinovief, and Kamenev decided to appeal to the rank and file of the party. The demonstration was received with indifference by the Moscow workers, and Trotsky was sent into exile in Siberia. In 1929 he was expelled from the Soviet Union, whence he traveled to several countries, ending up in Mexico where he was murdered (August 20, 1940) by Stalinist agents, recruited presumably among Spanish and Italian communist exiles.

Around the issue of collectivization of agriculture a new opposition emerged, led by Bukharin, who in 1927 had replaced Zinovief as leader of the Comintern, and Rykov, former premier of the Soviet Union. Both had previously helped Stalin against Trotsky. When the sixth world congress of the Communist International opened in 1928, Bukharin unavailingly quoted a letter sent him by Lenin: "If you chase all intelligent people who are not very pliable, and only keep obedient idiots, then you will certainly ruin the party." [1] In November 1929 the party declared that belonging to what was called the rightist opposition was incompatible with membership, and Bukharin also disappeared. The leadership of the Comintern was taken over by a committee of three, among whom was Molotov (1890-   ).

The final liquidation of internal opposition in the Soviet Union, however, did not take place until the late 1930's and was the direct result of the assassination of Kirov, the party leader in the Leningrad area, one of the trusted collaborators of Stalin and, from a communist point of view, a moderate. "It appears that supposedly loyal communists

[1] F. Borkenau, *World Communism* (New York: Norton, 1939), p. 337.

might hate the party leadership enough to commit murder," wrote at the time Mrs. A. L. Strong, an American admirer of all things communist; she justifies what she calls "the most spectacular series of treason trials in human history" on the basis that elimination of opposition was required in order to strengthen the USSR militarily in view of the coming World War II. No one knows exactly how many people were purged. According to S. N. Harper "in the course of the purge a couple of thousand people were executed"; and W. H. Chamberlin states that "almost a million members and candidates were expelled . . . between 1935 and 1937."

The official communist view was that "the trials showed that these dregs of humanity . . . had been in conspiracy against Lenin, the Party, and the Soviet state ever since the early days of the October Socialist Revolution." [2] Whatever the opinion about the trials, there is no doubt that by 1938 all organized opposition within the Communist party had been as efficiently destroyed as, in 1918-1921, the non-communist opposition in the Soviet Union had been liquidated. Russian communism had the monolithic strength which is the concomitant of the exercise of absolute power concentrated in the hands of a few leaders—in this case the members of the Politburo of the party.

The same process aiming at the elimination of all opposition, non-conformity, or deviation from the party line took place during that period in the communist movement of the rest of Europe. The twenty-one points approved by the second world congress of the Communist International had been clear enough. Had there been less intransigence, it is likely that a larger number of people would have joined the communist parties of the various countries. In Germany, for instance, out of 800,000 independent socialists only 300,000 decided to join the Communist party, originally organized around the 50,000 Spartacists. But smaller numbers were more than offset by greater cohesion. In Ger-

[2] *History of the Communist Party of the Soviet Union* (New York: International Publishers, 1939), p. 347.

many the struggle for leadership in the Communist party between Brandler, Maslow, Fischer, Thaelmann, and others ended with the victory of Thaelmann, who from the beginning had followed the Stalin line closely and had accepted unconditionally the open letter sent by the Comintern to the German Communist party on the need of absolute allegiance to Moscow. In France, Frossard, Souvarine, Loriot, Rosmer, and their followers joined the ranks of the dissidents. In Italy, Bordiga and his group were expelled from the party. The Norwegian group under Tranmael left the Comintern as early as 1923. In Poland, the numerous communists, who had taken their inspiration from Radek and Rosa Luxemburg and wanted to maintain their independence vis-à-vis the Russians were expelled.

Engels had maintained that "from the first moment of the victory . . . the distrust of the workers must not be directed against the conquered reactionary party but against . . . the bourgeois Democrats." Communists everywhere decided to do, before the ultimate triumph, what Engels had advised to do only after victory, therefore giving credit to what the German social-democratic leader Kautsky said of them: "the fundamental aim of the communists is . . . the destruction of democracy." Hand in hand with the process of internal clarification went the struggle against non-socialist progressive movements, and against groups ideologically close to communism but which rejected communist ways, particularly the non-authoritarian socialists.

The struggle against democratic tendencies was so severe that on several occasions communists helped rightist anti-democratic movements. This had been the case in 1920, when Kapp (1868-1922) revolted against the German republic; when Mussolini seized power in Italy (October 1922); and later, in 1924, when the communists refused to make common cause with the socialists, Catholics, and liberals who were trying to stop the fascist movement. It happened again when Pilsudski overthrew the democratic government of Poland (1926), and when Zankoff and his Macedonians rose in Bulgaria against the agrarian leader

Stamboliiski (1923). In France, in 1927-1928, the communists decided to drop the electoral collaboration which had existed with the socialists and the radical socialists, and helped the Right to achieve greater electoral successes. In Germany, in 1931, the Communist party, inspired by both Thaelmann and Neumann, worked along parallel lines to the Nazi party for the overthrow of the social-democratic government of Prussia. As late as the beginning of 1936, Spanish communists attacked collaboration with socialists and democrats aiming at saving the Republic.

The numbers of communists were not great, but in many countries they formed a group large enough to seize and hold power should occasion arise. At the sixth world congress of the Communist International (July-September 1928) it was stated that the total membership of the sixty-six parties represented was about 4,000,000, of whom the largest number (around 700,000) were in the Soviet Union, 300,000 in Germany, and nearly 100,000 in France. In relation to world population four million was an insignificant minority, but the four million formed a solid homogeneous group which an able and aggressive leadership could move in any desired direction. Lenin's policy of intransigence was to pay good dividends, and saved the communist movement from the weakness which internal divisions produced among the other branches of the socialist movement!

While the communist movement was undergoing this process of consolidation, attempts were made in the Soviet Union to apply the economic program of socialism. The fourteenth congress of the Communist party of the Soviet Union had already in 1925 approved a plan for the socialist industrialization of the country. But it was only after the fifteenth congress had expelled the Trotsky-Zinovief group from the party that the first Five Year Plan was introduced (1928 to 1932 inclusive). The decision to attempt the economic realization of the socialist program possibly was influenced by the war scare which had spread among the Soviet leaders. This was the result of the anti-communist policy adopted by the British government following the failure of the general strike in 1926; of the break between nationalists and communists in China; of a number of minor episodes such as raids against communist headquarters in Germany and the murder of Soviet representatives abroad; of the growing strength of anti-communist totalitarian movements; and of what appeared to be—until 1929—the strengthening of democratic capitalism in the United States. It was certainly affected by the realization that, in the long run, political tyranny cannot survive if economic forces are left free.

A remarkable economic recovery had taken place in the Soviet Union during the seven years of NEP (1921 to 1927). By the end of 1927 the economic wounds caused by the revolution and the civil war had been largely healed. But this recovery strengthened the position of groups of the population which were not in sympathy with communist ideals and practices, and represented a threat to the solidity of the regime. Moreover, collectivism and the use of the state to promote economic activities were essential elements of the Marxist-Leninist program, adopted by the Soviet leaders; and there was little doubt that the successful collectivization of the Soviet Union would strengthen communism to the detriment of the other socialist tendencies.

Stalin, now the undisputed leader of the Soviet Union and of the world-wide communist movement, had stated that the USSR was "50 to 100 years" behind the advanced countries, that an effort had to be made to make good that distance in ten years only. The Ministry of Economic Planning became, after the secret police, the most important element in the administration of the country. Little opposition could be expected in the industrial and commercial fields, where all large concerns had been nationalized before 1921 and where remaining small independent industrialists, craftsmen, and shopkeepers were easily absorbed into state-controlled organizations. More opposition was anticipated from the peasants, who from the beginning had shown greater sympathy for the socialist revolution-

aries than for the communists, who had also acquired ownership of the soil, and who still formed by far the largest
section of the population of the Soviet Union. Among them,
the rich peasants (Kulaks) represented about one million
households, or a little over five million persons. They were
not landlords or landowners but peasants themselves, sometimes (not always) receiving the additional help of hired
labor. Their wealth (a better house, a few more acres of
land, some livestock) was limited according to Western
standards, but it was considerable according to those of
other peasants. On January 5, 1930, the party leaders decided to eliminate the Kulaks. In what was a mass persecu-
tion, millions of people were uprooted; most ended in the
forced labor camps of northern Russia and eastern Siberia;
those who protested were jailed; many were shot. The party
acted so efficiently and ruthlessly that two months later
Stalin was able to call a halt to the process of elimination.
But the result was felt in the diminishing agricultural re-
turns that year and in the years following, and in the
famine which spread in several areas of the Soviet Union.

The physical aspect of many parts of the Union began
to change. With the help of several thousand foreign technicians (mostly Germans and Americans), coal, iron, and
oil fields were better exploited. Foreign equipment helped
to set up new factories. Moscow and Leningrad witnessed
a great increase in their populations. Large industrial cities
developed in the eastern Ukraine, in the Urals, and in western Siberia. The results of Soviet collectivism have inspired
differing appraisals. According to the British Marxist John
Strachey "the ever growing prosperity of the Soviet Union
enables the better paid workers to enjoy many of the
amenities and luxuries . . . reserved in England for . . .
the capitalist class." The American communist Earl Browder wrote that "during the First Five Year Plan, the rate
of increase in industrial production averaged 22 percent
annually; . . . in the United States . . . it never went
over 5 percent a year." But an expert in Russian affairs,
Leopold Schwarzschild, states for instance that "the ratio

between Soviet and American rates of growth in equivalent decades is 70 to 96 in iron, 588 to 1,389 in coal, 410 to 1,598 in copper, 38 to 1,320 in railroad construction, and so on."

Soviet economic achievements have been publicized and have struck the imagination of people who lacked the information required for a comparison between Soviet economy and Western economy. It can be stated, however, that Soviet achievements have been inferior to those obtained in several European and North American countries during the corresponding phase of industrial development. Lack of transportation, of skilled administrative personnel and of technicians, waste, and bureaucratic slowness—all prevented the complete realization of the Plan. The results, however, were sufficient to justify the satisfaction felt by Stalin and those who, like Molotov and Kuybishev, had collaborated with him. Through able propaganda which intelligently exploited a number of motives—from nationalism to fear, from devotion to an ideal to greed—a state of psychosis was maintained which induced large sections of the population to accept willingly the tyranny required by the execution of the Plan and the privations inflicted on the masses of the citizens.

THE STRUCTURE OF THE COMMUNIST ORGANIZATION

The communist movement as it exists today was molded during that troubled period which began with the year of revolution and ended with the consolidation of Stalin's control in 1927. Since the latter date it has been what Lenin wanted the Russian Bolsheviki to be: a highly disciplined movement with a maximum of cohesion achieved through the rigid centralization of authority and the elimination of all internal differences and conflicts. According to Carr: "[The] system of organization had long been described in party circles as 'democratic centralism,' a term intended to denote that double process by which authority flowed upwards from party cells in town or factory or village through intermediate local or regional committees, till it reached its apex in the central committee which was the organ of the sovereign congress, and discipline flowed downwards through the same channels, every party organ being subordinated to the organ above it and ultimately to the central committee." What happened between 1917 and 1927 was simply the logical development of the so-called democratic centralism. The leaders used their authority in order to eliminate from the communist parties all those who did not agree with them, and the parties were reduced to mirrors reflecting the will, aspirations, and policies of the leaders. Since 1927 the double process has been reduced to a single process by which discipline flows downward. This guarantees a maximum of cohesion, as the communist parties can be joined only by those who are willing to submerge their personality completely in the anonymous mass of loyal and faithful followers, and accept totally the "line" determined by the leaders. The efficiency of the communist parties derives to a large extent from the fact that they are not political parties in the accepted meaning of the term. They represent an all-embracing way of life which appeals to millions of individuals, not because of its economic or political implications but because the party members have a certain "character structure." From this point of view, joining the party is an experience equivalent to that of joining a church in times of great religious fervor.

The organization of a communist party is relatively simple. Theoretically at least, anyone who accepts unconditionally the principles of communism (whatever the interpretation may be at any given moment) may join. In many countries party membership is preceded by a probationary period. The basic elements are the cells, consisting of the communists who work in the same place (factory, mine, office, farm, etc.) or who live in the same neighborhood. Party members meet and discuss problems at the level of cells. In 1946 there were about 250,000 of these primary or local groups in the Soviet Union; no figures are available on the number of cells outside the Soviet Union.

Contacts between cells are few; those that do exist are rigidly controlled by the cell leader; hence it is extremely difficult, nay impossible, for any party member to look for other fellow members whose cooperation would be required to start a movement within the party. Through their leaders cells are grouped into district, provincial, or regional units, and these in turn into national parties. On the national level authority is still exercised nominally by central executive committees, but in reality—at least since 1926—by politburos. (The first Politburo was organized a few days before the October revolution and consisted of seven members.) As long as the Communist International existed, the national parties were subject to it. The Comintern governed through an executive committee which functioned permanently. Since the dissolution of the Comintern (1943), the functions of this committee have been exercised in practice by the Politburo of the Communist party of the Soviet Union, in collaboration with a few outstanding non-Russian communists (Rakosi, Thorez, Togliatti, etc.).

Present communist parties are hierarchical organizations similar in their internal structure to the German National Socialist party. The will of the leadership is identified with the will of the rank and file through the application of a simple formula: the rank and file elects the leaders, and the leaders determine who is to be in the rank and file. There may be dissident communists outside the party, but there is no room for a dissident communist within the party; once the dissident has been put outside the party there is nothing he can do to modify it. Only at the top level of leadership (the Politburo) is there a limited possibility for individual expression of opinion and for some independence.

Stalin has stressed emphatically the fact that the main function of the communist parties is to exercise dictatorial powers.[3] Sympathizers and critics have recognized that this

---

[3] "The dictatorship of the proletariat is substantially the dictatorship of the Party." Stalin, *Leninism* (New York: International Publishers, 1942), p. 34.

is the main feature of the political structure of the Soviet Union. The Webbs wrote: "The administration of the USSR is controlled to an extent which . . . it would be hard to exaggerate, by the Communist Party." S. N. Harper said: "The Soviet system is based on the one-party principle . . . oppositional rights receive no real protection." What, since the end of 1917, has been the position of the Communist party in Russia has become during the last few years the position of the communist parties in all the countries in which they have been able to seize political power.

There is considerable difference of opinion on the internal freedom within a communist party. One author, J. Somerville, a few years ago stated: "There is . . . opportunity for critical discussion regarding the effectiveness or shortcomings of the administration. . . . Major decisions of social policy are frequently preceded by widespread public discussions. . . . When the decision has been made . . . freedom of discussion in regard to the decision itself is considered at an end. . . . Freedom to teach against the objectives [of socialism] would jeopardize the freedom of the majority to attain a fuller life." But Borkenau, who has been intimately connected with the communist organization, says: "Since 1925 policy and administration became centralized in a few hands . . . ; since 1925 the central committees of the communist parties had been replaced by political bureaus in which the critical tendencies within the parties had no longer a voice . . . the autonomy of regions and districts was curtailed to the point of annihilation . . . the active membership was deprived, as early as 1926, of any possibility of exerting in practice its right to participate in the laying down of party policy." Whatever the opinion of communist sympathizers, it can be said that, as the result of expelling (or liquidating) those who disagree with the decisions of the party leadership, internal freedom within communist parties has been practically eliminated. In those countries where a communist party can make use of the state authority for its own aims, the freedom of the communists within a communist organization is as limited as the freedom of the non-communists outside. The intransigence, which in the early phase of the movement communists displayed towards non-communists,[4] has been transferred to the communists themselves. Concerning the internal organization, it is necessary to recognize that the concentration of power in the hands of a few individuals who have full authority over their followers helped the movement to achieve considerable flexibility of action, which is particularly useful when accompanied by a correct evaluation of the situation at any given moment.

The philosophical syntheses of Marx, Engels, and Lenin, as interpreted (with slight variations, additions, and corrections) by Stalin and his ideological collaborators, supply an easy explanation for all phenomena—human and non-human, past, present, and future. More important, they furnish a justification for whatever line of conduct [5] has been adopted, and provide each individual communist with an intellectual armor solid enough to make him impregnable to criticism. The importance of this armor in the over-all picture of communist strength should not be underestimated. The evidence gathered by the communist intellectuals to support their arguments, which is accepted uncritically by the rank and file, and the logic of their reasoning, have a considerable influence in maintaining the cohesion of the communist movement.

Stalinism, the present form of ideological communism, represents the adjustment of the principles of Marx (p. 8) and Lenin (p. 10) to a reality which developed somewhat differently from Marx's theoretical schemes. The terminology remains largely the same, but terms are often given

[4] "The history of the Party teaches that the victory of the proletarian revolution is impossible without a revolutionary party . . . irreconcilable towards compromises." *History of the Communist Party in the Soviet Union, op.cit.,* p. 353.

[5] "The power of the Marxist-Leninist theory lies in the fact that it enables the Party to find the right orientation in any situation." *Ibid.,* p. 355.

a different connotation, and, through an abuse of logical thinking, conclusions are drawn to prove that the structure of the Soviet Union and of the People's Democracies correspond to what Marx and Engels had in mind.

The best way to show what is irrational in Stalinism is to reduce a number of their own arguments to their simplest expression. A few examples will suffice:

1. "The administrative apparatus of a socialist economy can never become a new ruling class, because it lacks private ownership," wrote E. Browder, a former secretary of the American Communist party, who probably never heard of Praetorians, Mameluks, etc., all propertyless rulers exploiting property-owning classes, and who assumes that only private ownership creates a ruling class.

2. Socialism frees man from the bonds originating from economic shortages and economic restrictions; communists compel people to become socialists; *ergo,* communists make people free.

3. Opinions derive from interests; in a capitalist society there are different interests and therefore different opinions; socialism abolishes the difference of interest; *ergo,* in a socialist society there can be only one opinion. (Corollary: Whoever expresses a different opinion in a socialist society is an anti-social individual, therefore must be punished.)

4. The socialist state is the workers' state; by hurting their state the workers would hurt themselves; *ergo,* workers cannot be allowed to hurt themselves by engaging in strikes.[6]

5. War is the outcome of internal conflicts (in the case of a capitalistic society, the variety of interests); there are no internal conflicts in a socialist state; *ergo,*

[6] "Proletarian dictatorship . . . introduces universal obligation to labor, establishes the regime of labor discipline." N. Lenin and others, *The Manifesto of the Moscow International* (Manchester: The National Labour Press, 1919), p. 5.

no socialist state can engage in war, except a defensive one as the result of aggression on the part of a non-socialist state. (This argument has been used widely to prove that there was no communist aggression either in the case of Finland in 1939 or of Korea in 1950.)

This is the kind of reasoning that appeals not only to uneducated communists but also to legions of intellectuals. In analyzing the working of the communist mind, one should not forget that the communists are far from having a monopoly in irrational thinking: they simply do it better. Their exercises in semantics, reminiscent of some irrational scholastic practices in the Middle Ages, have helped to break down the barriers which reason's critical faculties may oppose to communist ideology. As happened in the nazi ideology, there is a seemingly strict logical process within the framework of an irrational system. The irrationality is covered up by faith; the logic satisfies the rational element in the intellectuals, who have played a greater role than the "toiling masses" in the development of the communist movement.

The concept of liberty as the intellectual and political expression of free will is unknown to communists, for whom "individual freedom . . . is conceived in terms of economic security. . . . Equal rights [mean that] . . . Soviet policy does not tolerate dissent in matters of substance. . . . Freedom of the press means that political powers take over all means of communication and proceed to control them." [7] Communists have a simple and uncritical faith in their system as the Gate to the Millennium.[8] Their materialism

[7] *Communism in Action* (Washington: U. S. Government Printing Office, 1946), pp. 133 *ff*.

[8] Under communism "a society can . . . witness the full unfolding of the marvellous potentialities of the human spirit." E. Browder, *What Is Communism?* (New York: Vanguard Press, 1936), p. 231. Communism can abolish poverty, unemployment, economic crises, wars, and prolong life, according to J. Strachey, *The Coming Struggle for Power* (New York: Covici, Friede, 1933), pp. 341 *ff*.

has helped them dispense with ethical principles and freed them from inhibitions which restrain the actions of most people. But materialism among communists has not led to cynicism; it has strengthened them as only a religious faith could have done.

The analysis of the structure of the communist organization explains the institutions introduced by communist parties in the countries in which they have seized political power. It would have indeed been strange if the communists had dealt with others more leniently than they deal with themselves! To the hierarchical party corresponds a hierarchical state, all the way from the citizens who are beyond salvation (members of the bourgeoisie, the clergy, the land-owning classes, etc.) and who are helped to disappear as quickly as possible, to the citizens who are slow to understand the meaning of salvation (the farmers), those who are saved because of their economic function (industrial workers), and the party members (reliable people whose duty it is to show others the way to salvation, and who must report all sinful acts and thoughts). Real democracy means the total transfer of power from the citizens to the rulers. Democratic centralism refers to the concentration of total power in the hands of the rulers, on the assumption that they express the revolutionary will of the triumphant proletariat. Authority from above is identified with authority from below through a combination of fear and bribes which induce those "below" to agree with those "above." As a communist party eliminates—and liquidates whenever possible—all "deviationists" (only the politburos have, collectively, the right to deviate), so an effort is made through the tools of the police state (arbitrary arrests and trials, firing squads, concentration camps, etc.) to eliminate all expression of dissent. The party functions 100 percent as a single unit; the citizens are regimented through state-controlled organizations in such a way as to function as a single unit. In the communist state all responsibility, all thinking, all decision-making is the monopoly of a cabinet which expresses the will of the politburo.

If by authoritarianism we mean the arbitrary use of authority on the part of those who hold power, and institutions which deprive members of an organization, or citizens of a state, of control over their leaders and rulers, both communist parties and communist states must be considered authoritarian. And if by totalitarianism we mean the exercise of authoritarian power not only in political relationships but in all fields of individual and collective activity, and the total subjugation of the citizens to the state, present-day communist states are governed by totalitarian regimes.

THE RISE OF FASCISM AND THE PHASE OF POPULAR FRONTS (1934-1939)

Chronologically, the fascist movement in Europe developed after the communist movement. It came into existence largely as an expression of the fear generated in many classes of the population by the triumph of the Bolsheviki in Russia and their reign of terror. Fascists maintained that communism had been bred by liberalism and that parliamentarianism facilitated its diffusion. Hence they turned even more violently against liberalism and democracy than against communism.

In March 1919, in Milan, a small group of people of different political tendencies formed a union or *fascio*. Insignificant during the first two years, it soon grew so strong that its leader, Benito Mussolini (1883-1945), was able through a show of force to seize the government of Italy (October 1922). After a short experiment in coalition and a violent struggle against their opponents, during which several thousand people were killed, the fascists established a totalitarian regime in November 1926. The name *fascism* was given to similar movements which soon after developed in various European countries.

The fascists shared the communists' contempt for democratic procedure and for liberalism, the conviction that their movement was entitled to make use of ruthless violence for the achievement of their aims, a policy leading to the strengthening of the state through the elimination of all dissent and opposition, and the concept that the group (in their case, the nation) is superior to the individual. They differed from the communists mainly on economic policies and, theoretically at least, on the question of nationalism *versus* internationalism, not in the aspiration toward totalitarianism. The fascists (in Italy in 1922 and ten years later in Germany) came chiefly from the ranks of the lower middle classes (which in some European countries constitute as much as one third of the population). These had not participated in the struggle for freedom during the nineteenth century, and among them newly acquired education had developed a strong nationalistic feeling. If the lower middle classes provided most of the human element for the development of fascism, the capitalistic groups (rich landowners, bankers, and industrialists) were generous in providing financial assistance for a movement which claimed to protect private ownership of property.

The triumph of the fascists in Italy was followed by the establishment of a military dictatorship in Spain (1923), by the seizure of power by Pilsudski (always more of a nationalist than a socialist) in Poland (1926), by the development of the movement of the Heimwehr in Austria (1927), and by the establishment of a royal dictatorship in Yugoslavia (1929). In Germany the first feeble attempts (1923) on the part of local fascists (the National Socialist or Nazi party) failed miserably, and for several years nazism vegetated obscurely as one of the many extremist groups in the country. The economic depression of the early 1930's gave impulse to the movement, and it came into power on January 30, 1933. This was followed by the establishment or consolidation of dictatorships of the Right in every country east of Germany and Italy, between Estonia and Greece, with the one exception of Czechoslovakia.

The rise of fascism did not at first unduly worry the communist leaders, who saw in it another enemy of the hated democratic regime, an enemy who was considered less formidable than liberalism. The growth of national

NEUTRALITY (1939-1941)

The Popular Front experiment had not been an unqualified success. In Spain it had strengthened the communists for a while, but it had also deepened the cleavage between communists and non-communist anti-fascists (democrats, social democrats, syndicalists, anarco-syndicalists, etc.). In France it fizzled out after the one-year cabinet (1936-1937) of the socialist Léon Blum. Nowhere in the countries of central and eastern Europe had it shaken the dominant dictatorships of the extreme right.

From a communist viewpoint, there had been three main failures: (1) The Popular Fronts had not checked the advance of fascism in Europe; at the beginning of 1939 fifteen out of twenty-seven non-soviet European states, with nearly 250,000,000 inhabitants, were under fascist or semi-fascist dictatorships. (2) The Popular Fronts had not enabled the various Communist parties to dictate their own policy to the parties with which they collaborated; if anything, their lack of confidence in the communists had increased. (3) In the international field the policy of collective security through the League of Nations carried out by the Commissar for Foreign Affairs, M. Litvinov (1876-   ), had not improved the relations between the Soviet Union and the two main states of western Europe, the United Kingdom and France. At the Munich conference (September 1938) the fate of Czechoslovakia, a state friendly to the Soviet Union, had been settled by the governments of Germany, Italy, France, and Great Britain without as much as an invitation to the Soviet government to be present.

According to Marxist-Leninist theory, capitalist countries [9] should have combined in an attack against the

[9] Communist terminology is often confused and contradictory. Apparently communists now divide the non-communist world into capitalistic countries, and backward areas exploited by the former. Fascist corporate economy, British controlled economy, and American free-enterprise economy are all "capitalist."

socialism in Germany, however, was a different affair. In the free elections of the early 1930's, the number of communist voters had increased from 3,000,000 to 6,000,000. But the number of Nazi votes had increased from less than 1,000,000 in 1928 to over 14,000,000 in 1932, and at the presidential elections of that year Hitler (1889-1945) received 17,000,000 votes. Fascism was no longer the political expression of a frightened minority of nationalistically minded property owners. Fascism could be as much of a mass movement as communism, or more. Gottwald (1897-   ) wrote in 1934 of the parties of the Second International: "The facts convict these hyenas and traitors, prove that the Austrian Socialist Party has brought the proletariat under the knife of fascism." But the other leaders of the communist movement saw the danger, and the result was a change in policy of fundamental importance: "Instead of class struggle, cooperation with the bourgeoisie. Instead of the Soviet system, eulogy of democracy. Instead of internationalism, nationalism." To symbolize the change in policy, the leading position in the Comintern, which had been vacant since the expulsion of Bukharin, was filled by G. Dimitrof (1882-1949), the Bulgarian hero of the *Reichstag* fire trial in 1933 (after the end of World War II, dictator of Bulgaria).

First came agreements between the Soviet Union and other countries such as France and Czechoslovakia, and the application by the Soviet Union for membership in the League of Nations (1935). This was followed, on the national level in various countries, by a reversal of the policy of aloofness and an attempt to develop "Popular Fronts" in collaboration with socialist parties and with middle-class leftist parties. In France, communists and socialists had already participated in common manifestations on February 12, 1934—at the time when the Republic was threatened by rightist organizations. By 1935 there was collaboration between socialist and communist youth organizations and trade-unions. When, in 1935, non-communists launched the idea of a Popular Front in France, the Communist party accepted it enthusiastically, and the result was the remarkable leftist electoral victory of 1936. In Spain—where the military dictatorship of De Rivera had been replaced by a republican regime—the initial opposition of the communists to a Popular Front was quickly reversed, and there was also in 1936 an electoral victory for the left (which preceded by a few months the nationalist revolt under Franco). The Popular Front policy was rejected in the countries in which the socialist parties were controlled by liberal-minded elements (Scandinavia, Great Britain, Holland), and by the democratic socialists who earlier had formed the Second-and-a-half International. Elsewhere it became a reality. In dictatorial countries it led to agreements between communist and socialist undergrounds or exiles, who were often joined by the radical wing of the middle-class liberal movement.

The Spanish Civil War (July 1936-March 1939) provided a testing ground for the effectiveness of the Popular Front policy and for the ability of the communists to take over the leadership of a coalition of which they were part. At the time of the rising in the Asturias (northern Spain) against the republican government in 1934, communists and some non-authoritarian socialists had collaborated. It was then that Dolores Ibarruri, known as *La Pasionaria,* acquired the reputation which made her one of the leading communists in the world. At the elections of February 1936 the communists had only a few deputies elected in the Popular Front list. But after the Franco rising the Communist party probably did more, in relation to its small numbers, than any other political group to organize the resistance against the military leaders supported by the Catholic hierarchy, the capitalists, the majority of the peasantry of western Spain, the Moors from Spanish Morocco, and the German and the Italian governments. While fighting against Franco's troops, the communists tried at the same time to eliminate all opposition to themselves in republican territory. In the rising of March 1937 in Barcelona a number of anarco-syndicalists were killed, as well

as numerous members of the anti-communist socialist group, the Unified Marxist Workers' party (POUM). The position of the Communist party in Spain was strengthened by the failure of the French and British governments to help the non-communist enemies of Franco, and by the material help sent by the Soviet Union to the forces of the Spanish republic. The communists organized most of the international brigades which played a prominent part in the defense of the capital, and which provided valuable fighting experience for communists from all over Europe.

Earlier another, and in the long run much more important, civil war had begun in the Far East, in China. Events there, however, followed a different pattern. After the triumph of the nationalist faction in the Kuomintang and the expulsion of communist organizers, a few centers of communist resistance had been set up in various parts of China. A soviet government had been organized in 1928 in the counties on the border between Hunan and Kiangsi, south of the Yangtze Kiang; another in the hilly area where the provinces of Anwei, Honan, and Hupeh meet; and a third in the northwestern provinces. With the strengthening of the Kuomintang, efforts, which were partly successful, were made to occupy these areas. In October 1934 the communists south of the Yangtze Kiang began—under the leadership of Mao Tse-tung—the "Long March," which ended a year later in the northern province of Shensi. There, at Yenan, they established their headquarters and carried on intermittent warfare against the nationalists, who had been pressed by Japanese attacks since 1931. The renewal of Japanese attacks against China proper in 1937 had, for the Chinese communists, an effect similar to that of the triumph of nazism for European communists; they decided to modify their opposition to the nationalists and to build a common front against Japan—then the Far Eastern equivalent of European fascism. Attempts at cooperation between communists and nationalists became more numerous after the clashes between Japanese and Russian troops along the Manchurian border in 1938.

socialist state, in this particular case the Soviet Union. The communist leaders proved once more their ability to act independently of their theory by "freeing" the Germans for a war against Great Britain and France. While a British military mission sent to Moscow in the summer of 1939 was making no headway, conversations were being carried on by Soviet leaders with representatives of the German government. The conversations led to the mutual non-aggression pact of August 22, 1939. Ten days later the Germans, freed from the fear of war on two fronts, attacked Poland (September 1, 1939) and World War II started.

The new orientation of the Soviet Union and of the communist movement had not come unexpectedly. It caused, however, a certain amount of tension within the communist parties and among fellow travelers. There were many resignations in countries outside the Soviet Union, but not enough to weaken appreciably the communist parties then waging a decided campaign against the "imperialistic" war in which France and the British Commonwealth had engaged against Germany and her European friends. What remained of Popular Front policy was swept away, and the communists reverted to the pre-1934 policy of virulent attacks against "bourgeois" liberal democracy, and against democratic socialists as betrayers of the proletariat.

For the first time since 1922 there was an expansion of the territories ruled by communists. The Soviet Union took advantage of the war to bring various European territories under its control, thus strengthening the communist positions. On September 17, 1939, Soviet troops invaded Poland. As the result of agreements with the nazis, over half the territory of the former Polish republic, with more than one third of the population, was annexed to Byelorussia and the Ukraine, two republics of the Soviet Union. According to one observer, "the process of sovietization in the Polish areas taken by the Soviet Union was carried out more or less along the pattern of the NEP. . . . There was no immediate and forceful collectivization of agriculture. Small traders were allowed to continue business. Landlords, large manufacturers, large merchants, former officials and some clergy, were handled roughly. . . . Some evacuation of industry was carried out." On November 29, 1939, Soviet troops invaded Finland, but found greater resistance than had been expected. The war ended, however, on March 2, 1940, with a Soviet victory. Finland gave up some territories which, together with former Russian districts, were erected into a new state of the Soviet Union. During the summer of 1940 Soviet troops invaded the three Baltic republics of Estonia, Latvia, and Lithuania. According to Harper "the Soviet technique in taking over these small countries was . . . to combine invitation with pressure. . . . Between 200,000 and 300,000 recalcitrants are said to have been sent east." Under the threat of war, Rumania was compelled to surrender the province of Bessarabia and the northern part of Bukovina, where a majority of the population was Ukrainian. These actions were justified in communist eyes by the necessity of strengthening the Soviet Union while the "capitalistic" nations were fighting it out.

In the British Commonwealth communist parties were relatively unimportant, and did not appreciably weaken the British war effort. In France the Communist party, which by then was polling around 1,000,000 votes, sabotaged French military preparations with determination and success. (The desertion of the communist leader Thorez was a small but significant episode.) When the Germans invaded Yugoslavia and then Greece (April 1941), the communists of the two countries did not move, and resistance against the invaders was at first carried out mainly by nationalistically minded members of the ruling classes, with the support of sections of the peasant population.

The switch from an anti-fascist policy to what amounted to a policy of benevolent neutrality toward German fascism could not weaken the position of the communists in the Soviet Union, where all opinion-making media are operated by the government. Official propaganda emphasized the annexations of 1939-1940, which satisfied the nationalistic aspirations of the Slavic majority of the population of the

USSR. Outside the Soviet Union, small numerical losses were more than compensated for by the increased cohesion within the movement. Party members and sympathizers who had stood the shock of the nazi-communist pact of August 1939 were evidently people in whom the leaders could have unlimited confidence.

THE PHASE OF NATIONAL FRONTS (1941-1945)

The German attack upon the Soviet Union (June 22, 1941), and the defeats of the Soviet armies on the eastern front during the first few months of war, caused an abrupt and radical reversal of communist tactics. This time it was no longer a question of Popular Fronts, of agreements with other leftist movements. The threat was grave, and the very existence of the Soviet Union was in jeopardy. The communists were now willing to collaborate with anyone who was against the Germans and the nazis. The "imperialistic" war became a war for freedom and for democracy. National Fronts became the slogans. And in every country —legally where it could be done, underground elsewhere (in most of Europe and in the Japanese-occupied Far East) —the communists were instrumental in bringing about a greater integration of anti-nazi forces.

In the Soviet Union concessions were made to nationalism and to religious organizations. Nationalism was still deeply rooted among the Great Russians, the Ukrainians, the 20,000,000 Turkish-speaking people of the Union, and many smaller national groups. Concessions to nationalism were not difficult, considering that the faction which, under the leadership of Stalin, had taken over the control of the Communist party had always been less internationally minded than the other factions. Concessions to religion aimed at acquiring the support of the large section of the adult population which had never accepted the official atheism of the Soviet regime, and of the small section of the younger generation which was religiously inclined. The Orthodox Church acquired what many considered a position of privilege. After a twenty-year lapse, the Moslems of the Union were allowed to resume pilgrimages to Mecca in 1944. More important, in order to allay the suspicions of non-communists, it was decided to dissolve the Comintern (May 1943). The official interpretation of this act was that now every national communist party was on its own, and that there could no longer be the suspicion of "orders from Moscow." Many thought, instead, that the Comintern had simply gone underground.

Under different names, National Fronts were organized in most parts of occupied Europe, engaging in sabotage and guerrilla warfare. In France the communists collaborated with General de Gaulle, with democratic socialists, with the Catholics, and with the radicals, and were the animating spirit in the French Council of the Resistance. In Italy they were active in promoting the Committee of National Liberation in which many political tendencies were represented. In Greece, where the communists had received 100,000 votes in 1938, a short time before their party was outlawed by General Metaxas, they promoted the formation of the National Liberation Front (EAM) which included the Communist party, the Agrarian party, the Democratic Union, the Democratic Radical party and, for a short while, the Socialist party. In Yugoslavia, under the leadership of Tito (Josip Broz, 1892-   ) was formed the AVNO (Anti-Fascist Council of National Liberation) in which communists, socialists, agrarians, Catholics, radicals, and democrats were represented. Toward the end of the war a Fatherland Front was formed in Bulgaria, including —besides the communists—socialists, agrarians, the Zveno group, and others. Another Fatherland Front was organized in Albania. In Poland a National Front was formed under the inspiration of Polish communist leaders residing in Moscow; collaboration of all anti-nazi forces, however, proved to be impossible here because of the deep hatred the nationalistic underground felt for the Soviet Union, on account of their participation in the downfall of Poland in September 1939.

Where non-communist anti-nazi groups refused to collaborate with the communists, new groups with the same name, but led by communist sympathizers, were organized, and civil war broke out at times between communists and anti-communist opponents of nazism and fascism. This happened, for instance, in Yugoslavia, where Serbian nationalists under General Mihailovitch were accused of fighting against Tito rather than the Germans; in Greece, where the EAM was opposed by the guerrillas organized by General Zervas; in Poland, where the large underground which recognized the authority of the government in exile in London was subjected to the attacks of the communists, who refused to cooperate in the Warsaw rising of September-October 1944 led by General Bor. In other countries (France, Italy, Belgium, Holland, Norway, Czechoslovakia) the tension between communists and anti-communists within the resistance movement was generally kept under control, and they were spared the additional sufferings which were caused elsewhere by inter-resistance fighting.

Thanks to better cohesion, better discipline, and more experience in underground organization and guerrilla warfare, the communist parties acquired a predominant position in most resistance movements, although their numbers were often smaller than those of the non-communist underground and guerrilla fighters. They were instrumental in preventing the consolidation of German rule in occupied Europe, and gave valuable military help to the Allies fighting on the eastern front, in Italy, and, later, on the western front. During the resistance period European communists strengthened their parties, acquired in many countries a military organization, and found themselves in possession of large stocks of arms and ammunition, partly taken from the enemy, partly sent to them by the Western Allies. Their willingness to cooperate with non-communists, their energy, the moderation of political, economic and social programs which they put forth during this period, and the prestige of the Soviet Union, combined with the state of chaos and confusion in which the end of the war found most of Continental Europe, enabled the communists to widen considerably the base of their popular support.

In the Western Hemisphere, communists redoubled their activities. In several countries they were strengthened by the arrival of communist refugees from Europe; everywhere, except possibly in Argentina, they profited by the admiration the world felt for the stoical endurance and the strength of the Soviet peoples. In the United States and Canada a determined attempt was made—under the guidance, in many instances, of Soviet representatives—to infiltrate the various branches of the public administration, the military forces, labor unions, and youth organizations. The small communist groups which for some time had existed in the Latin American countries enjoyed a freedom of action unknown before. In Mexico, Cuba, Chile, and Brazil they were able to build or to take over political and labor organizations. In every country of the Western Hemisphere, the communists were sponsoring causes which appealed to the liberal, radical, and progressive elements of the population: the end of racial and religious discrimination, the diffusion of education, social legislation, government intervention in economic affairs to correct the abuses of capitalism, and the like. To many, communism—during this period —appeared to be just another political movement, willing to play according to the rules of parliamentarian democracies. Why consider it differently from the other parties?

In the Far East, nominal collaboration was established between nationalists and communists in China, although the communists refused the fusion of armed forces which alone could have guaranteed the final unification of Chinese territory. In Korea, in Indochina, in Burma, in the Philippine Islands, in Malaya, communist organizers tried to imitate what their colleagues had achieved in most of Europe. Their success was less spectacular, but by the time the war came to an end they had nuclei strong enough to influence the changes which were taking place.

Since the revolution of 1911 there had been in China a nearly uninterrupted succession of internal and external conflicts, and when the war ended the Chinese nation was exhausted. The pressure of the West had caused a landslide involving every aspect of Chinese life, thought and religion as well as economics and politics. The institutions inherited from past centuries, and the traditional values on which they had been based, had weakened. The relationships between individuals and classes which had made sense in what had been a paternalistic authoritarian society had now become meaningless. A deep economic transformation was taking place; a wretched and unstable urban proletariat filled the new industrial cities which had sprung up along the coast and in the northeastern provinces; contacts with a new wealthy class made the peasants increasingly aware of their own misery. The family, the village community, and traditional education were no longer capable of holding the individual. The situation was not very different outside China proper. Whatever the appearances, Korea and Manchuria had been Japanese colonies; the defeat of the Japanese left a political vacuum which no local force was able to fill. South of China the Japanese invasion had dealt a severe blow to British, French, and Dutch colonial administrations. The political and economic structures built by Europeans in the course of generations were swept away during the three and a half years of Japanese control. Chaos and disorder reigned. From Java to Manchuria in 1945 the situation was not dissimilar to that which developed in Russia in 1917 after the collapse of the czarist regime. Here was a chance for a small but militant and aggressive group to seize control; it would have been against the theory and practice of communism to let the golden opportunity pass.

3

Communism Since 1945

THE end of World War II in Europe (May 1945) found much of the Continent in a state of anarchy. Nazi rule had been the equivalent of a revolution. Millions of people had been killed; tens of millions had been uprooted; for years suffering had been part and parcel of life. Political and economic institutions had collapsed. Beliefs, values, ideas around which had been organized the social structure of many European nations had either disappeared or their influence had weakened considerably. Nazi-fascism had suffered a crushing military defeat; there were still plenty of individual fascists, but they were isolated units and hence incapable of action. Conservatism and capitalism as organized social forces were weakened by the fall of fascism. Liberalism had withered to an extent which would have been unthinkable a generation earlier: liberal parties were only a faint reflection of what they had been and life seemed to have gone out of them. Democratic socialism was still numerically important, but its inability to check the advance of authoritarianism during the previous twenty years had exposed its fundamental lack of energy—the result largely of the conflict between (*a*) the desire to establish collectivism, which requires an authoritarian framework, and (*b*) a genuine attachment to liberty, which requires some autonomy at least in the pursuit of economic activities. Nationalism was still a powerful emotion, though less so than in the recent past, but had little organization. In many countries, the postwar political vacuum was only partially filled by several varieties of Christian socialism or Christian democracy. Under conditions of disorder, poverty, confusion, deluded hopes, and intense hatreds, communism found an atmosphere favorable to its further development.

From a communist viewpoint, the most important result of the war had been the strengthening of the Soviet Union. In May 1945 Soviet troops were in total occupation of what, before 1938, had been ten independent states in Europe: Finland, Estonia, Latvia, Lithuania, Poland, Czechoslovakia, Hungary, Rumania, Bulgaria, and Albania; also parts of Germany, Austria, Norway, and the Danish island of Bornholm. Some Soviet troops were also in Yugoslavia, where power was firmly held by the communist leader Tito. Soviet troops were soon withdrawn from northern Norway and Bornholm. The annexations of 1940 were confirmed through agreements among the Big Powers reached at Teheran, Yalta, and Potsdam. To them were added sections of northeastern Germany and southeastern Czechoslovakia. This represented a total of 185,000 square miles with nearly 25,000,000 inhabitants, of which about 40,000 square miles with nearly 8,000,000 inhabitants had never belonged to Imperial Russia. In the Far East no one objected to the annexation of the former Chinese territory of Tannu Tuva (1944). Manchuria, Korea north of the 38th parallel, southern Sakhalin, and the Kuril islands were occupied by the Soviets, who annexed the two last-named territories (about 20,000 square miles and 500,000 inhabitants).

During the war there had been considerable talk on the part of people who did not understand the dynamics of the communist movement, about a possible "liberalization" of the Soviet regime—in the sense of allowing some freedom of expression and some internal opposition—and of the concession of the reality of self-government to the sixteen republics of the Union. There had been mention of differences between the Communist party, the bureaucracy, and the armed forces, of tension between the ruling oligarchy and the new middle class of managers and professional people, accounting for 5 or 6 percent of the population, of dissensions within the higher levels of the communist oligarchy. The fact that possibly as many as 200,000 Ukrainians and 80,000 Moslems from the Caucasus and Soviet Central Asia, out of several million P.W.'s, had accepted to fight for the Germans had been interpreted as an indication that the cohesion of the Soviet Union was not so great as had been supposed in the late 1920's. With the war's end there was, however, no indication that the internal solidity of the Soviet Union had declined or that the authority of its leaders was challenged. Not everyone in the Union was happy about the development of socialism,[1] but the official line remained the nation's line.[2] Five ethnic groups were deprived of what the Soviets call national and cultural autonomy because of the sympathy which a majority of their people had shown toward the German invaders. Measures were taken in 1946 to stamp out what appeared to be a recrudescence of nationalism in the Ukraine. When elections took place, the customary plebiscite went to the candidates chosen by the communist organizations.

(After 1945 the backing of the Soviet Union was, even more than before 1939, instrumental in guaranteeing the influence of communist parties in every corner of the world. It is reckoned that the Soviet Union lost over 7,000,000 dead in the war against Germany and that the war cost her the equivalent of nearly $200 billion. In spite of her losses, the Soviet Union was stronger than ever. Interna-

[1] "The despotic and bureaucratic administration of Russia's economic life cancelled out the benefits that we expected a collectivized economy to bring. . . . The Russian workers receive a much smaller share of the product of their toil than the workers in any capitalist country—smaller than they received under the czar." A. Barmine, *One Who Survived* (New York: G. P. Putnam's Sons, 1945), p. 313.

[2] "The Soviet worker has seen his country's living standards continually improve. . . . The Soviet people rely [on socialism] to attain a living standard equal to that of the United States." W. A. Mandel, *A Guide to the Soviet Union* (New York: Dial Press, 1946), pp. 313-315.

tionally, the Soviet Union enjoyed a better position than Russia had ever had. In 1914 there had been seven Great Powers in the Eastern Hemisphere; in 1945 only one remained beside the Soviet Union—a considerably weakened United Kingdom. Militant communism was encouraged by the first postwar Five Year Plan, with an emphasis on heavy industry that could be interpreted as a willingness to use violent methods if peaceful ones failed.

The eight European states not annexed by the Soviet Union and at present (1952) within the Soviet sphere of influence (Albania, Bulgaria, Czechoslovakia, Eastern Germany, Finland, Hungary, Poland, Rumania) cover an area of about 560,000 square miles and have a population of nearly 100,000,000, with total national incomes equivalent to about half the national income of the Soviet Union. Postwar developments in six of these eight countries (Eastern Germany and Finland being the exceptions) followed a similar pattern, as did also a seventh state, the communist but not Soviet-controlled republic of Yugoslavia. When, as the result of Soviet military victories, the Germans were compelled to evacuate or to surrender, the victorious Russians or their allies (such as the Yugoslav partisans) put power into the hands of a coalition government composed of representatives of the groups which had participated in the anti-nazi National Fronts during the war. The main feature of these coalition governments was the occupation by a communist of the post of Minister of the Interior, who, in European countries, has direct control over the police. Non-coalition parties, under the pretext— not always true, as in the case of Poland—that they had aided and abetted nazism, were suppressed or prevented from exercising any influence, because of the impossibility of using means of communication (press, radio, cars, meeting places, etc.), all of which were strictly controlled by the government. At the same time a fairly considerable section of the economy was nationalized, in order to make producers totally dependent on the government.

Having acquired full control of the police, the communists proceeded to the second phase of development: the weakening, through arrests and threats, of the non-communist members of the coalition showing signs of independence. In the six Soviet-controlled countries and in Yugoslavia this phase occupied most of 1946 and part of 1947.

The third phase was characterized by the structural reorganization of the state, and the consolidation of political communist monopoly. The appearances of the coalition were usually kept up, a few well-chosen crypto-communists (such as Fierlinger in Czechoslovakia) representing non-communist groups. All organized opposition was liquidated. Fundamental liberties (personal liberty, freedom of expression, of conscience, of teaching, of association, of movement, etc.) were abolished or restricted to the extent of suppression. Rapid advances were made in collectivization, transforming most citizens into wage or salary earners whose earnings were dependent on the government. State monopoly was established over education, the press, and all other means of communication. Forced-labor camps were opened or expanded; recalcitrant citizens, or those who might become so, were arrested; a few were sentenced to death and shot or hanged in order to scare those who still harbored resentment against the communist dictatorship. This final phase was reached in Albania, Bulgaria, Rumania, and Yugoslavia by the end of 1947. Poland, Czechoslovakia, and Hungary reached it in 1948, Eastern Germany in 1949.

The speed of the communist advance was partly regulated by internal conditions. In Czechoslovakia there was a relatively high standard of living and of education, a lively nationalism, and, in some sections of the population, a fairly strong democratic feeling. In Eastern Germany there remained a strong nationalism, but twelve years of ruthless nazi repression had weakened all democratic forces to the point of near-extinction. In the other countries there was little democratic strength or tradition. Poland, Hungary, and Rumania had been ruled in the period between the two wars by the corrupt and weak descendants of what had once been a virile and responsible feudal class; Bulgaria, Yugoslavia, and Albania by despots who had little root among the peasant population of the three countries. Once the old political structure had been swept away, the only political force which could have checked the advance of communism was agrarian socialism, represented in Poland by the Polish Peasant party led by Mikolajczyk; in Hungary by the Smallholders party, under inexperienced leadership; in Rumania by the followers of Maniu; in Yugoslavia by those of Macek; and in Bulgaria by the movement led by D. Dimitrof and N. Petkov. Agrarian socialism lacked organization; the communists were efficiently organized and were helped by the presence of Soviet troops. The struggle could hardly be called such, as agrarian socialism, despite its numbers, was nowhere able to put up a serious fight. It collapsed as easily in these countries in 1945-1947 as its Russian counterpart, the Socialist Revolutionary party, had collapsed in 1918-1919.

In four countries, either a majority (as in Poland, in Czechoslovakia, and in Hungary) or a large minority (in Yugoslavia) of the people had been reared in the beliefs and institutions of Roman Catholicism. In these countries the Catholic Church was the only organization that seriously tried to put up a certain amount of resistance; it fought, however, a rapidly losing battle. The arrest and trial of a few members of the hierarchy (cardinals, archbishops, and bishops) was enough to intimidate a good many of the clergy. Through the nationalization of wealth, the clergy were reduced to the servile position of all bureaucrats. By the end of 1950 it was clear to many thoughtful Catholic leaders that Catholicism in Soviet-controlled Europe was condemned and would be weakened to the point of insignificance. Non-Catholic religious bodies (Orthodox in Rumania, Bulgaria, and Yugoslavia; the Protestant minority in Hungary; the Moslems in Albania and in Yugoslavia) offered even less resistance than the Catholic Church, and accepted the position of obedient cogs in the new dictatorial structures.

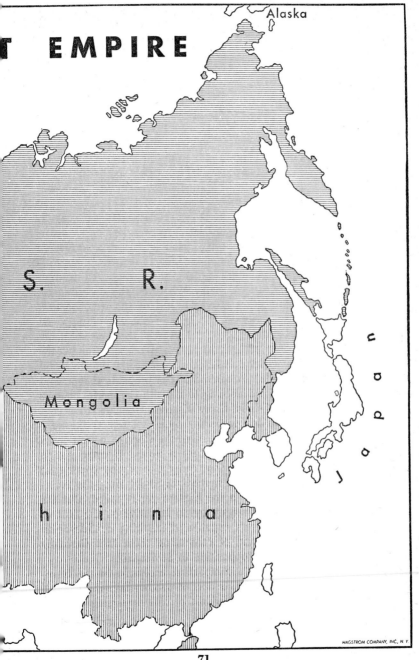

EMPIRE

Alaska

S. S. R.

Mongolia

China

Japan

Events in the Soviet zone of Germany followed a somewhat similar pattern. At first, as in the other zones, four political parties had been authorized by the victors: Social Democratic, Christian Socialist, Communist, and Liberal Democratic. Taking advantage of the usual split within the socialists, between those who stressed free institutions and those who advocated collectivism, the Soviet authorities were able to bring about a fusion between the latter and the communists under W. Pieck. This led to the establishment of the Unified Socialist party. The Social Democratic party, which anti-communist socialists would have liked to organize, was outlawed. At the end of 1947 J. Kaiser and other Christian socialists were forced to abandon the leadership of the Christian socialists and were replaced with pro-communists. Liberal democrats, unwilling to accept communist orders, were compelled to find refuge in the Western zones. Whatever the appearances, four and a half years after the end of the war, Eastern Germany was solidly in the grip of the communists. As under the nazi regime non-nazis had faced the choice of being liquidated sooner or later or acting as nazis, so under the new rule most citizens, whatever their secret thoughts and aspirations, decided to conform. It is probable that a consideration which had nothing to do with the merits or evils of communism, helped many Eastern Germans to accept willingly what in any case they could not reject: the hope that by serving the Soviet Union, the German nation could be allowed to reunite, and that a united German nation might one day achieve the leadership of the communist world. It is true that the immediate Soviet aim—the incorporation of all Berlin in the Eastern zone—failed. But the failure was not followed up by an initiative on the part of the anti-Soviet Powers capable of inspiring confidence in Eastern Germany, and of convincing them that Germany could be reunited in opposition to Soviet will.

Finland represents an important exception in the European Soviet sphere. The conduct of public affairs there is still based on democratic procedure; private ownership of property is recognized; freedom of expression and of conscience are a reality. Finland had been an exception also during most of the 108 years of czarist rule. Its relative autonomy fulfills a role similar to that entrusted by the nazis in 1940-1945 to Denmark, the show place of nazi tolerance destined to attract would-be sympathizers and friends. Finland is too small and too weak to represent a threat to the Soviet Union; it is unlikely that it could be used as a military base by far-away potential enemies such as the United States or the British Commonwealth. It provides a useful channel of communication with the Scandinavian states. If the need should arise to form a coalition with noncommunist states, the Soviet leadership could assure doubtful states that their position would be as good as that of Finland. On the other hand, what has been done in the other satellite countries could be achieved in Finland in a very short time.

The close relationship between all these countries and the Soviet Union was made clear in June-July 1947, when those invited rejected the invitation sent by the British and French governments to participate in a common effort for the economic recovery of Europe through the Marshall Plan. Under the leadership of the Soviet Union, steps were taken for an economic integration through a system of trade agreements (the Molotov Plan), aimed at increasing economic exchanges between the various states, at reducing their dependence on Western capital and markets, and at achieving a considerable amount of industrialization through their own resources.

What the Molotov Plan was supposed to achieve on the economic level, the Cominform aimed to realize on the intellectual and political levels. The central control established by Stalin's group in the 1920's on all communist movements had weakened during World War II. This weakening could easily lead to the development of heresies, or "deviations," in the communist parties outside the Soviet Union. To maintain orthodoxy and conformity, central power had to be institutionalized, while at the same time it had to be supplied with the means to enforce its control. This led to the re-establishment of the old Comintern in the form of the *Cominform* (Communist Information Bureau), organized at a meeting held in Poland in which the leaders of eight European parties, including those of Italy and France, participated. As had been the case nearly thirty years before, the communist leadership felt that greater cohesion and coercion were required for the successful achievements of communist aims and aspirations.

It is probable that when the Cominform was established, the Soviet authorities already had misgivings concerning Tito. For over a quarter of a century he had been a loyal party official. The accidents of war had made of him a leader strong in his own right. The withdrawal and surrender of the Germans had left him in complete control of Yugoslavia—a country located on the western border of the Soviet sphere of influence, enjoying therefore the possibility of direct relations with the Western Powers, and endowed with natural defenses and considerable natural resources. The diffidence toward Tito led the other members of the Cominform to accept Belgrade, the Yugoslav capital, as the headquarters of the organization—the best place from which to keep an eye on a potential rebel. We do not yet know the exact reasons which led to the rupture between Tito and the Cominform in 1948 when, in view of the forthcoming struggle with the Western Powers, greater discipline was demanded of all communists. It is possible that Tito rejected Soviet plans for the rapid collectivization of the Yugoslav economy; it is possible that Tito wanted to launch an attack against Greece, or Italy, or Austria, and that the Soviet leaders did not yet want to become involved in a major conflict; it is possible that the realization of a Balkan federation (wanted by Tito) would have led Balkan communism into the paths of socialist agrarianism, hated by the Soviet leaders because of its democratic features; or again, there may have been nothing but the clash of strong personalities.

Whatever the reason, the break occurred, and Tito and his advisers (among whom were Pijade and Kardelj) found themselves with the necessity of formulating a communist ideology different from that of the Soviet. Leninist-Stalinist communism was based on the twin concepts of centralization and power from above. Yugoslav communists, in self-defense, began to stress the concepts of decentralization and power from below, thus moving one step toward the fundamental Western concepts of the individual's autonomy and responsibility. Decentralization and power from below meant, politically, giving reality to Yugoslav federalism; economically, it meant placing a hierarchically organized economy with considerable autonomy and responsibility in the hands of local bodies and workers' organizations. Yugoslav communism is, institutionally, a dictatorship; but its ideological basis—contrary to what happens in the Soviet Union and in the Soviet-controlled countries—is no longer a totalitarian one. There is, therefore, in Yugoslavia a conflict between theory and practice, which may in the long run weaken the existing dictatorship and possibly bring about a revision of communist institutions. The effect of Titoism on the communist movement outside Yugoslavia has so far been slight; a few "liquidations" were enough to scare would-be imitators. However unlikely, one should not exclude the possibility that—in case the Soviet Union suffers a loss of prestige and influence due to internal political or economic difficulties, or to international complications—national and federalistic communism may one day appeal to many who at present accept Russian imperial and autocratic communism. The acceptance of Titoism would in that case probably have as great an influence on the communist movement as the acceptance of the fundamental political and intellectual tenets of liberalism had on the socialism of western and central Europe in the nineteenth century.

In Asia, the Soviet attempt to create a system of buffer states controlled by local communist groups strongly held in hand by Russian leadership, met with varying success.

Starting in the west, much pressure was at times exercised on Turkey by the Bulgarians and, along the northeastern border, by Soviet Armenians who claimed Turkish provinces once inhabited by Armenians. As the result of the severe anti-communist policy followed by the government of the Turkish republic since its establishment shortly after the end of World War I, there was no organized group in Turkey capable of lending its support to the activities of local or foreign communists, and the Soviet attempts to intimidate the Turkish republic failed.

During World War II, Soviet troops had occupied the northern section of Iran (Persia), while the British occupied the southwest. The Soviet troops were to have left the country a few months after the end of hostilities, as the British did, but when the time came they did not move. Combined British-American pressure, exercised through the United Nations, induced the Soviet government to order evacuation of Iran in 1946. This was done in such a way as to leave behind in Azerbaijan—the most populous province, in the northwestern section of the country adjoining the Soviet Union—a communist-controlled provincial administration. A few months later the central government of Iran sent an expeditionary force and after brief fighting was able to restore its authority. Since then, waves of nervousness have swept Iran each time that Soviet troops were moved along the border. At times Kurdish tribesmen, apparently under communist influence, agitated against the governments of Irak and Iran, but without immediate success. More favorable to communist interests was the tension between Iran and Great Britain which grew out of the nationalization of the British-owned oil fields, in 1951.

Further east, in Sinkiang, the largest and westernmost province of China, the USSR had exercised a good deal of influence over local tribes during most of the 1930's. A withdrawal had taken place during World War II, when Soviet leaders sought to inspire confidence in the members of the nationalist government who then ruled over most of non-occupied China and were bent on fighting Germany's ally in the East, Japan. At the end of 1947 Soviet influence had been re-established through the support of anti-Chinese Turkish tribes. Today Outer Mongolia, whatever its internal structure, may be considered as much a part of the Soviet Union as the five Soviet republics of central Asia. Most of

Manchuria had been occupied by Soviet troops in 1945; their successive withdrawals were effectuated so as to leave most of the country in the hands of Chinese communists.

As the result of an agreement reached between the American and the Soviet governments at the end of the war, Soviet troops occupied Korea north of the 38th parallel, a territory of about 50,000 square miles with a population of around 12,000,000. Under the supervision of Soviet agents, Korean communists acted as their colleagues in the European satellite countries had done. Opponents and potential opponents were destroyed; power was concentrated in the hands of the hierarchically organized Communist party; state monopoly was imposed over means of communication and of education; much of the wealth was nationalized; and a few reforms were introduced in order to give the inhabitants the impression that from now on they would be properly looked after by the state. With feverish activity, and good results, a relatively large army of probably not less than 200,000 men in fighting units was organized, commanded mostly by Koreans who had been trained militarily either by the Japanese or by the Chinese communists. Encouraged by the American declaration in January 1950 that Korea was not within the American line of defense, the communist government of northern Korea invaded southern Korea on June 25, 1950, thus taking the first step in the policy of limited aggressions conducted by subordinate communist powers, which has probably been adopted by the leadership of the communist movement as one of the best means to achieve eventually a total communist victory.[3]

[3] No one can say at the beginning of 1952 what the impact of the Korean war on the future developments of communism will be. A few facts, however, stand clear: (1) The communist attack brought untold suffering to the Korean nation but it failed in its immediate objective. (2) It convinced the American nation at the time that force was an important factor in the communist expansion and that force had to be checked by force. (3) It absorbed much of the armed power of the Chinese People's Republic and weakened for a while the pressure of Chinese communism over southeastern Asia. (4) By compelling the Soviet Union to divert part of its industrial effort to the war in the Far East, it weakened for a while Soviet pressure in Europe, particularly against Yugoslavia.

As in the case of eastern Europe and Korea, the communist success in China was due mainly (1) to the intelligent use of violence by a strongly integrated and highly cohesive minority group, with a fanatical belief in the righteousness of its cause. To this factor, inherent in the communist movement itself, must be added others which had nothing to do with the Chinese communists: (2) the Japanese aggression which dislocated China, exhausted large sections of the population, and prevented the nationalists from concentrating all their efforts on unifying the country; (3) the occupation of Manchuria by Soviet troops and the surrender to the Chinese communists, at a critical moment, of large stocks of Japanese arms and ammunition; (4) the inability, due partly to unwillingness and partly to inefficiency, on the part of the nationalist regime to carry out an agrarian reform and to maintain law and order, sadly lacking in many areas under their control; (5) the pressure exercised by the United States government over the nationalists with the aim of inducing them to collaborate with the communists—pressure based on the assumption, stressed by numerous writers on Far Eastern affairs, of a fundamental difference between Russian and Chinese communism.[4] In the state of chaos in which China found itself, power was bound to fall into the hands of the best-organized minority. Only foreign intervention could have kept in power a divided and inefficient minority like that represented by the Kuomintang.

[4] The theory that Chinese communism is inherently different from Russian and Western communism derives from the priority attributed by Marxists and many non-Marxists to economic factors. According to economic determinists, a communist regime which looks after the peasants and derives its main support from the peasantry must act politically in a different way from a communist regime which cares mainly for the industrial workers and derives its main support from the urban proletariat. This view is contradicted by those who, like myself, believe that the policy of a government depends on the political institutions within which it operates. A dictatorship acts as a dictatorship, whether it draws its support from the peasantry or the urban proletariat (or, for that matter, from the military, the capitalists, or any other class).

Throughout the war against Japan, which lasted, with brief intervals of peace, fourteen years (1931-1945), relations between nationalists and communists in China had remained strained, in spite of several attempts at collaboration.[5] During the last stages of the war, the nationalists had insisted on the unification of the armed forces as the price for eventual collaboration in the government with the communists. While the war was in progress, the communists had been concerned about building up their own strength, and had no intention of giving up what they knew to be the most important element in the struggle for final success. In the summer of 1945, the communists had about 1,000,000 men under arms, and were in control of most of the northern provinces; their guerrillas took over districts evacuated by the Japanese before the nationalists had time to arrive. The occupation of Manchuria by Soviet troops in August 1945 influenced the course of events more than anything else. A considerable economic expansion had been effected by the Japanese in Manchuria; in August 1945 a treaty had been rashly signed between the Chinese government (which was under the impression that it was implementing American policies) and the Soviet government. The treaty recognized on one hand the independence of Outer Mongolia and limited Soviet rights in Manchuria and, on the other, Chinese sovereignty over Manchuria. When the Soviet troops withdrew, most of the vacated localities were taken over by the communists. Two years after V-J Day, the communist forces numbered 2,000,000 men.

[5] Before the end of the war, spokesmen for the communists and the nationalists used to express similar views: "We are willing to cooperate with the Kuomintang not only while the war lasts but afterwards." Mao Tse-tung, as quoted by G. Stein, *The Challenge of Red China* (New York: Whittlesey, 1945), p. 114. "If the Chinese communist party . . . and the Kuomintang are left in their present position, most likely there won't be any civil war." Dr. Liu, quoted in H. F. MacNair, *Voices from Unoccupied China* (Chicago: Chicago University Press, 1943), p. xxii. On the other hand, the theory and practice of communism show that no communist party can accept (except as a last resort in a desperate situation) subordination to a higher authority. Communists either control or oppose.

Fighting between nationalists and communists varied in intensity, but never stopped entirely. At first there were nationalist offensives, such as that which led to the occupation of Yenan, the capital of the communist area. When fresh and newly equipped communist divisions took the offensive, the nationalist military leaders made the strategic blunder of trying to hold Manchuria, a region far from China Proper; their best troops were encircled and compelled to surrender. Defeat followed defeat, and by the end of 1949 the whole of China, with the exception of the island of Formosa (technically until the signing of the peace treaty with Japan in 1951 a Japanese possession, and then the refuge of the nationalist government), was in the hands of the communists, who proclaimed a People's Republic with the capital at Peiping. Following the example set by the states of eastern Europe, China nominally has a coalition government; in reality, it is a one-party police state run by the highly centralized Communist party in which authority comes from above. No opposition or dissent is tolerated; all means of communication, material and other, are controlled by the government; parts of the economy have been nationalized, the rest is rigidly controlled by the government which holds the monopoly of economic initiative. While the masses in China care little for communism or anti-communism (and have no voice or possibility of expressing their views), communism is likely to appeal to a much larger minority than democracy ever did. The concepts of liberty, of individual responsibility and dignity were never strong in the Chinese tradition; traditional Chinese society had possessed an excellent system for the control of the human mind and had developed political despotism to a fine art. The communist regime takes over where China left off in 1842, with the addition of economic control to political and intellectual control.

By the end of 1951, the communist movement, which fifty years before was only an idea in the minds of a few hundred or a few thousand radicals, had achieved complete power over an area of between 13,000,000 and 14,000,000 square miles (one fourth of the land area of the globe, excluding the Antarctic), inhabited by more than 750,000,000 people (one third of the world's population), with national incomes equivalent then to more than $100 billion. The extraordinary success of communism can only be compared to the Graeco-Macedonian conquest of western Asia in the fourth century B.C., to Rome's conquest of the Mediterranean in the second century B.C., to the Islamic expansion of the seventh century, to the empires conquered in a few years by Attila, Genghis Khan, and Timur.

It is impossible to predict whether the communist empire will follow the destiny of the Macedonian, Roman, or Mohammedan empires—which built cultures that survived—or the destiny of the ephemeral empires conquered by Attila and Timur. The present reality is that it exists, and that it represents the greatest threat to the values, concepts, and institutions for which Western civilization stands.

THE POSTWAR EXPANSION OF COMMUNISM: OUTSIDE COMMUNIST-CONTROLLED AREAS

In Europe, the greatest communist successes were achieved in France and Italy. This was partly the result of the excellent organization built up by the communists during the period of nazi occupation, and of their activity in the resistance movement. In France, at the first elections held in 1945, the Communist party, which used to receive about one vote in seven before World War II, improved its position considerably and obtained the support of more than one fourth of the voters. During the following years its voting strength increased to 29 percent; at the elections of 1951 it was still more than 25 percent, in spite of economic recovery and the reorganization of anti-communist forces. In the 1951 parliament the communists formed the second largest group. For nearly three years after the liberation of the country they participated in coalition governments, except for the short-lived government led by the socialist Léon Blum (Dec. 17, 1946-Jan. 22, 1947). In

May 1947 the socialists—accusing the communists of sabotaging the efforts of the government from the inside and of making use of their collaboration to strengthen their own party—supported by the Catholics of the *Mouvement Républicain Populaire* and by the liberals, decided to form a government without communist participation. Later in the year an anti-communist rightist movement was organized by General de Gaulle; it received a plurality of votes in the municipal elections of 1947, and in 1951 sent to the parliament the largest single bloc of deputies.

In Italy, communist ministers sat in coalition governments from April 1944 to May 1947. At the general elections of June 2, 1946 (the first free elections in the country since 1921), they received just under one fifth of the votes. Under the leadership of Togliatti, party membership had increased already to more than 2,000,000, the Italian Communist party being the largest outside the communist empire. In May 1947, the leader of the Christian Democratic party resigned as Premier and, entrusted with the formation of a new cabinet, formed a homogeneous one of Christian Democrats and independents which was strengthened at the end of the year by the inclusion of representatives of small democratic groups. Contrary to what was happening in France, a majority of socialists decided in favor of strict collaboration with the Communist party, from which they became almost indistinguishable. At the national elections of April 1948, and again at the local elections of 1951, communists and socialists voted together; it is supposed that the strictly communist vote increased by about 50 percent, from 4,000,000 to 6,000,000 voters. In the parliament the communists form the second largest group. "Deviation" was kept strictly under control; a few intellectuals left the party and two deputies were expelled. This caused a number of speculations concerning Italian "Titoism," but only a negligible influence was exercised at first by the dissidents over the masses of the faithful. In April 1951 the party leadership announced a total membership of over 2,500,000.

The collapse of nazism brought about a limited revival of the communist movement in the non-Soviet zones of Germany, where more than seven tenths of the German people live. In 1932 the Communist party had been the third largest, ranking after the nazis and the social democrats. After the defeat of 1945 the communists were competing with the Christian socialist (or Christian democratic) movement, with the social democrats, and the liberals. Under conditions of freedom of vote guaranteed by the occupying forces of the United States, Great Britain, and France, the communists could nowhere obtain more than a small fraction of the vote. In the *Länder* of the three zones, the largest percentage of votes was received by the Christian democrats (particularly in the Catholic areas) or the social democrats. The communists made a determined effort to forge ahead, but with remarkably little success. The local elections of 1950 showed that they had lost ground.

In Austria, at the general elections which took place after the end of the war, the communists received less than one vote in twenty. The prestige of the small Austrian Communist party was at first strengthened by the presence of the Soviet army of occupation; the prestige later weakened almost to the vanishing point.

In the Scandinavian countries, in Holland, Belgium, and Luxemburg, the communist parties at first improved their position in relation to the prewar period. But they soon lost what little extra influence they had gained and remained small and relatively unimportant. Political leadership was retained in the hands of social democrats or Christian socialists. In Switzerland and in the British Isles also, the communists remained small and noisy minorities with little weight in political affairs. In Spain and Portugal they existed only as underground groups.

In Greece there had been little or no evidence of communist participation in the war between Greece and the Axis (October 1940-April 1941). After the nazi attack on the Soviet Union, the communists took active part, together with other groups, in the resistance and, after the withdrawal of the Germans in October 1944, attempted to overthrow the Greek coalition government of which they had been members. The revolt was put down by the combined efforts of British troops and Greek anti-communist forces. The communists and various pro-communist groups refused to participate in the elections of March 31, 1946. Allied observers—British, American, and French—expressed the opinion that, had the communists participated in the elections, they would have received at the most one third of the votes. They decided, instead, on guerrilla activities, favored by the mountainous nature of the country and by its extensive frontier with Bulgaria, Yugoslavia, and Albania, all controlled by communists. By the end of 1946 considerable guerrilla activity had been carried out under the military leadership of Markos Vafiades (1906-?). During 1947 attacks were made against many towns and villages in the northern provinces. A commission sent by the United Nations to investigate the situation reported that the communist-led guerrillas, estimated then at 15,000 men, were receiving help from the communist regimes of Bulgaria, Yugoslavia, and Albania. The deterioration of the situation in Greece and the possibility that the conflict between communists and anti-communists would lead to further complications and the establishment of a communist regime, induced the United States government to take a direct interest in the internal affairs of the country (March 1947). This was deeply resented by the USSR and helped to increase the rift between the United States and the Soviet Union. A coalition government of royalists and liberals tried to calm the tension inside Greece by granting an amnesty to the guerrillas. At the end of December 1947 a provisional government was formed by the communists in the area of Mount Grammos. The reorganization of the Greek forces under the supervision of American experts, and Tito's defection from the Soviet camp, contributed toward bringing the civil war to an end in 1949. The 1951 elections showed only a small section of the population in favor of communism.

Browder as chairman of the party, and his replacement
. Z. Foster. As the result of Soviet tactics in the United
ons, the aggressiveness of the Soviet Union and other
nunist-controlled countries, and the increased con-
sness of the fundamental and incompatible principles
mocracy and communism, a wave of anti-communism
the United States and led to the expulsion of com-
ts from a number of organizations and positions. The
gle was particularly strong in the labor field, where
unions "witnessed the most determined upheaval
t communism." Public authorities dismissed com-
ts and fellow travelers from the federal and state
istrations. By the end of 1947 the communists had
themselves more or less isolated in the American
. They tried a carefully staged come-back in 1948,
h a new version of the "Popular Front" represented
e newly established Progressive party, nominally
by the former Vice President Henry Wallace. The
ssive party polled a little more than 1,000,000 votes,
ch probably only half or less were votes of com-
s or convinced fellow travelers. These numbers suf-
further decline in 1949 and 1950, when the evidence
et aggressiveness and communist determination to
world control became too strong to be ignored by
ut honest former admirers. At the elections of No-
1950 the last fellow traveler in Congress lost his

legal status of the Communist party represented
the important problems facing the administration,
s, and the American nation at the beginning of the
half of the century. Should the party be outlawed?
be considered on the same level as other political
functioning and willing to go on functioning within
ework of democratic institutions? Some legislation
curbing communist activities was passed, mainly
but the problem of the position of the Communist
d only partially been solved with the Supreme
ecision in June 1951 to recognize the validity of

Communist progress was considerably slower in the
Moslem countries than in Europe. By the time World War
II ended there were active, although not large, communist
groups in French North Africa, particularly in Algeria,
and in some of the states of the Near East and the Middle
East (Syria, Lebanon, Iran). Religion was a strong barrier
against the spread of communism. Mohammedanism is not
in itself more anti-communist than Christianity, but on
the whole religion probably means more to the Moslems
than to the Christians. Moreover, the influential groups of
the population, the upper and middle classes, are for the
most part nationalistic. The attempt of the USSR to create
a pro-Soviet attitude in the Moslem countries by allowing
Soviet Moslems to travel outside the Union did not give
appreciable results. And in 1947, on the pretext of danger
of epidemics, Soviet Moslems were again forbidden to make
their pilgrimage to Mecca. In Turkey a strong nationalistic
regime has practically stamped out native communist organizations. In Iran communists are still relatively few, in
spite of the progress they made in the areas occupied by
the Soviet Union between 1942 and 1946; their numbers
may have increased in 1951, following the tension between
Iran and Great Britain. In Syria the Communist party was
outlawed at the end of 1947, but seems to be still fairly
active. In the two most populous Moslem states, Pakistan
and Indonesia, there has been little communist agitation
so far. In Pakistan it has been remarkably absent, despite
the favorable conditions brought about by the transfer of
power from the British to the Moslem League in August
1947. In Indonesia a small communist organization played
second fiddle to the nationalists of various tendencies who
led the movement for the final overthrow of Dutch rule;
attempts made by communists to achieve through force
what they could not achieve through persuasion were repressed by the new government in 1949-1951, which ordered
wholesale arrests of communists and presumed communists.

A similar situation exists in the Union of India, where
a small Communist party has little weight and influence.

Many leaders of the Congress party had been in sympathy with the Soviet Union, just as some of them had favored the Axis during the war, simply because the USSR and the Axis were against Britain. Having achieved independence, that sympathy waned—except in the case of a few intellectuals—while strong anti-communist forces (such as orthodox Hinduism and nationalism) have appeared on the scene. Communist agitation was repressed successfully and the Communist party was outlawed in some of the States. A situation which might have helped a communist minority to seize power could have developed if the peasant masses had felt too acute dissatisfaction toward the existing regime; agrarian reforms were, however, carried out in Uttar Pradesh, the most populous State, and if they become general, agrarian unrest may be avoided.

At the beginning of 1951 a different situation existed in the easternmost peninsula of southern Asia. For centuries Burma, Annam, and, to a lesser extent, Thailand, Laos, and Cambodia, had gravitated within the orbit of Chinese civilization; in British Malaya Chinese immigrants formed the largest group of the population. The disruption of European direct or indirect control caused by the Japanese invasions and occupation during World War II, the weakness of traditional social structures, and the impulse provided by small groups of active and convinced communists had made of communism, in which most radical aspirations were confluent, a primary problem. The revolt against the French and against native traditional authorities in Viet-Nam (formerly the empire of Annam) was organized by Ho Chi Minh, one of the ablest Asian communists. A common boundary with China after the end of 1949 gave the Viet-Namese communists a considerable advantage over their opponents. In Burma and in British Malaya the communists were less numerous than in Viet-Nam; what they lacked in numbers they made up in energy and activity. In these countries internal warfare had been waged almost uninterruptedly since 1946. The situation looked none too promising in the other three (Thailand, Cambodia, and Laos).

In the Philippine Islands, com[
threatening the democratic experim[
pinos had embarked. Communists [
thousands, but they were favored b[
Filipinos to understand that their e[
not be quickly solved. In Japan, li[
by communist organizations after t[
tary autocracy in 1945 brought a[
victory, despite the number of prop[
Soviet Union who returned to Japa[

In the Western Hemisphere, the[
the United States and Canada ha[
opposition since the end of the war[
the party, as she had done previo[
covery of a spy ring of communist[
intelligence of the Soviet Union, tl[
a more careful watch on the activit[
Their numbers have remained sm[
filtrate Ukrainian-Canadian and [
munities through nationalist and re[
not yield appreciable results. In s[
communist influence remained st[
labor movement showed little tende[
The only communist deputy in tl[
was unseated as a result of his tr[
his place was taken by a liberal.

In the political life of the Unit[
of the war, communists remained [
if highly vocal, element. In spite [
termination, they lost most of th[
in the 1930's and during the war[
of collaboration, they had been al[
number of organizations.[6] In Fe[
"palace revolt" led to the expulsi[

[6] "More than seventy nation-wide org[
by the [communist] party to which [
lured to give them a 'respectable' front.[
American Communism (New York: D[

the Smith Act under which the leaders of the American Communist party were being tried. It is safe to say that some confusion still exists in the minds of many Americans as to the true relationship between democracy and communism.

South of the Rio Grande, communism was often stronger than in the English-speaking countries. In Mexico, the Communist party, led by D. Encinas, was small but for some time acted as the leader of Latin American communism. As previously noted, a number of European refugees and exiles had strengthened it. Under the leadership of V. Toledano, an attempt was made to develop a Latin American labor movement sympathetic to the Soviet Union. But a reaction set in, and in January 1948 a meeting took place in Lima, Peru, called by the anti-communist labor unions of various countries.

In Cuba, the communists controlled the labor movement to a considerable extent, but, just as in Mexico, they were unable to win the support of large groups of the population. In Guatemala, the few communists enjoyed an ephemeral influence at the end of the 1940's.

In Brazil, the Communist party, outlawed during the first Vargas regime, showed unexpected strength at the elections of 1946, polling about 600,000 votes. Its leader, C. Prestes, became a member of the Senate. Communism was strong, particularly in the more industrialized southern Brazilian states, where a large percentage of the population was not of Portuguese or mixed Portuguese-African descent. In 1947 the Brazilian government declared the aims of the Communist party to be incompatible with the constitution of the country, and the party was outlawed. At the same time tension arose between Brazil and the Soviet Union, which led to the severing of diplomatic relations between the two countries.

There was similar tension between Chile and several states in the Soviet area, because of the part diplomatic officials had played in fomenting strikes in the territory of the former. At the 1946 presidential elections the communists had participated in a Popular Front which included socialists and radicals. The Popular Front polled a majority of votes; the new president, a radical, tried to govern the country with a coalition cabinet which included the communists. The experiment lasted only a few months, after which the other parties compelled the communists to withdraw from the cabinet. As in European coalition governments, the communists had used tactics detrimental to the partners in the coalition and had made the smooth operation of democratic procedure difficult.

In Argentina, the Communist party opposed both the Péron regime and the democratic opposition. Its influence, however, remained small, although it enjoyed the advantages of more competent leadership than in other South American states. Elsewhere in Latin America, communism rarely reached the proportion of a major political factor.

In the spring of 1947 some figures were published concerning the membership of communist parties in most countries of the world. It is of interest to quote them in order to obtain an idea, however vague, of how many communists there are. By major cultural areas the totals were:

Soviet Union, 6,000,000, or about 3 percent of the population; rest of Continental Europe (excepting the nine smaller democracies), 9,450,000, or about 3 percent; nine smaller European democracies, 340,000, or about 1 percent; English-speaking nations, 167,000 (United States, 74,000, or 0.5 percent, British Commonwealth, 93,000 or 1 percent); Far East and India, 2,123,000, or about 2 per thousand (mostly in China); Latin America, 502,000, or a little over 3 per thousand; no figures were supplied for the Moslem areas of the Near East or Africa.

It is difficult to say how reliable these figures are. Various experts have maintained that since 1947 the number of communist party members has declined considerably in Western countries. According to non-communist sources, there had been in four years a decrease of 50 percent in Great Britain and Germany, of over 25 percent in France and Italy. Communist sources, and election results, usually indicate a smaller decrease. In some of the eastern European countries many party members were expelled after 1949. In the Far East (China) party membership has presumably gone up. Everywhere convinced communists (including fellow travelers) formed a highly cohesive group: there may have been anything from ten to twenty million in 1951. They constituted the core of the communist movement and should be distinguished from the tens of millions who supported communism for various reasons, but had neither the communist spirit nor mentality.

WHAT NEXT?

It is a well-known fact that groups held together purely by common aspirations, goals, and interests (both material and non-material) are not as cohesive and influential as those composed of people who cooperate not only because of some common aspiration, goal, or interest, but also because of similarities in their mental make-up and personalities. This similarity is particularly important in the early stages of the development of a social movement. Contemporary movements, from democracy to socialism, from fascism to communism, from nationalism to internationalism, have originated in groups of individuals characterized by a certain way of thinking and certain attitudes. In most modern societies one can find people who are potentially democrats or socialists, fascists or communists, nationalists or internationalists; if they are isolated, their influence is nil or negligible; if they are integrated in groups of their own, they may be able to influence the whole society.

Lenin's function was a catalytic one. He gathered together a few kindred spirits; once a nucleus was formed it attracted others, first among the Russians and, after 1917, also among non-Russians. Potential communists existed before 1903 and 1917; thanks to the political, economic, and intellectual crises of the first half of the twentieth century, those whom Lenin had helped to find themselves joined forces, formed groups (the communist parties), and became a movement. Wherever they achieved power (by the end of 1950 over one third of mankind), they used the force of the state to mold in their own image as many as possible of their fellow countrymen, through a monopoly of education and the media of communication. Those whom they could not mold, they either destroyed ("liquidated," in communist parlance) or kept isolated by depriving them of the possibility of establishing relations with one another.

For an understanding of the developments which are likely to take place within the communist movement, it is necessary to keep in mind the main aspirations of the "faithful" and their interpretation of the world in which they live. Similar aspirations and interpretations can be found in other movements: it is their combination in a well-integrated system that constitutes communism. This system can be summed up in the following points:

1. The primary stimulus to action for a communist is an emotional one: the consciousness and horror of economic suffering, both made possible by the freeing of human beings from various forms of political, economic, and intellectual bondage brought about by liberalism during the last two hundred years, either directly (where it triumphed) or indirectly (where it weakened and caused the collapse of traditional authoritarianism). How this is reconciled with the practice of ruthless cruelty is explained in Point 21.

2. On the practical level the communist desires to end the exploitation of man by man. *Exploitation* is understood exclusively in economic terms of a relationship between individuals within a certain social structure (see Point 10 below). Political and intellectual domination do not exist *per se;* if the employer is the impersonal representative of the collective will, there is no domination and no exploitation.

3. All individual and collective activities must be directed toward the goal of greater material welfare (more goods, more leisure, etc.). Communists here simply give greater emphasis to an aspiration which is also stressed by Western liberalism.

4. Points 2 and 3 can be achieved only through the establishment of a collectivistic society in which private ownership of the means of production has been abolished. This has been proved "scientifically" by Marx through the analysis—conducted dialectically—of human history.

5. Point 4 is so important that all means are legitimate which lead to the establishment of collectivism. Among these means *violence* is a most important one.

6. The triumph of collectivism requires the previous conquest of the state, which is nothing but organized violence.

7. Once the communists have conquered the state, no limit can be put to the exercise of their power. For the good of the toiling masses, there must be a dictatorship.

8. From this it follows that all power must be concentrated in the hands of the communists—that is, the state must be totalitarian. Communists reject categorically the fundamental liberal principle of the division of power. In a communist state there can be no separation between political power, economic power, and religious power, nor division within political power. Any autonomy that may exist is not a right of individuals or groups, but a concession made by the state for purely administrative reasons.

9. The universe is so ordained that collectivism is inevitable. The identification of their aspirations with a supposedly universal law has been of fundamental importance in strengthening the communists in the difficult stages of their political struggle. It is equivalent to the Crusaders' conviction that they were carrying out God's Will.

10. The reality of the universe is represented exclusively by Matter, which is inherently endowed with certain features and operates on the basis of inherent laws. The communists deny emphatically any supernatural level of existence; God therefore does not exist.

11. The universe can be understood only through application of the dialectical principle corresponding to the process through which Matter changes and is transformed.

12. Reason is an attribute of Matter, like movement, energy, etc. The communists reject the identification of

the universe with the spirit as emphatically as the concept of God.

13. Man is, of course, part of Matter. He is like clay, and as clay he is molded by the laws inherent in Matter itself. There is no such thing as an independent reason or an independent will; the individual's autonomy simply does not exist.

14. Man is molded by economic forces which act on the basis of laws inherent in the world of economic phenomena, and which are part of the laws of the universe.

15. As reason and will are merely attributes of Matter and expression of laws determining the universal material process, liberty does not exist. Man can only do what he is compelled to do by economic forces.

16. As morality, or evaluation of what is good and what is evil, and choice between them, implies liberty, and liberty is nonexistent, so also morality is non-existent *per se*. What human beings call morality is an attribute of Matter and varies with the structure (economic organization) of the Matter.

17. The non-existence of morality *per se* leads the communists to deny the autonomous existence of the law as a system of moral principles, the observance of which is enforced by the state. The denial of law leads to the denial of the concept of the citizen, who is a physical individual endowed with rights and duties—that is, with moral elements.

18. Human reality is represented by categories (economic groups and social classes), and not by individual units included in the group; individual units have no more autonomy than the cells in the human body. Communism rejects categorically the "nominalism" which characterized Western thought from the eleventh to the twentieth centuries, and from which sprang humanism, Protestantism, and liberalism.

19. The liberal assumption of the self-sufficiency, autonomy, and responsibility of the individual is false. Communists are those who have been economically conditioned

to discover the truth of human developments; the others are either too limited and cannot discover the truth (and must therefore be led) or are economically determined not to accept the truth (and must therefore be destroyed).

20. The group, existing *per se,* has total control—political, economic, or religious—over the individual. The communist mind cannot conceive of majority and minority in a group; it is always "the proletariat," "the bourgeoisie," the "clergy," not "the proletarians," "the bourgeois," "the ministers," among whom some may follow one tendency and some another.

21. The individual who refuses to conform to the group to which he belongs is a cancer, a diseased element, and must therefore be destroyed. This postulate is important for an understanding of how communists can combine the concern for human suffering (Point 1) with the practice— and the theory [7]— of such disregard for human life as has rarely been witnessed in the history of mankind. In "nominalistic" terms, communist humanitarianism belongs to the level of abstractions (the collectivity) and is therefore compatible with cruel ruthlessness on the level of reality (the individual). What matters is the welfare of the proletariat, not of the proletarians. The mental approach here is similar to that of the nazis, who were indifferent to the sufferings of millions of Germans because what mattered to them was only the nation or race. Neither communists nor nazis can understand the Christian concepts of love and charity for individual man.

22. In broader terms, heresies and "deviations" are diseases in the social body and must therefore be extirpated. A healthy society requires that all its members conform completely to the type required by the society itself.

From these twenty-two points it is easy to see that communists are compelled by their own beliefs and by their

---

[7] "In principle we have never renounced terror and cannot renounce it." Lenin, quoted in E. H. Carr, *The Bolshevik Revolution, 1917-1923* (New York: Macmillan, 1951), p. 156.

understanding of the world in which we live to enforce political despotism and intellectual dogmatism. There is nothing in their attitude which has not been experimented with—at times fairly successfully (from their point of view)—by other movements; what is new is the possibility, supplied by technological progress, of exercising greater control over the individual than ever before.

The question is often asked whether communism can change its internal structure and go through a process of liberalization, or whether it is chained to authoritarianism to such an extent that all communist states must be police states. Both communist and non-communist Western intellectuals have often maintained that authoritarianism is only a passing phase, the result of capitalistic and imperialistic pressure; that, with the consolidation of communist regimes and the weakening of internal opposition and external aggression, an era of liberty will be introduced and the withering away of the state, foreseen by Marx, will become a reality. In theory most things are possible. On the basis of recent historical evidence, however, this optimistic view of the future of communism seems to be based on a number of misconceptions concerning certain fundamentals, particularly the nature of collectivism, the communist ideology, and the influence of political institutions brought into existence by communism.

Experience shows that discipline and authority are required for the proper functioning of economic enterprises. In a capitalistic society there are hundreds of thousands, or millions, of different enterprises. Because of their multiplicity, because of conflicting interests separating industry, agriculture, trade and credit, also separating employers and employees, management and labor—in other words, because of the division of power characteristic of democratic societies, the enforcement of authority and discipline is limited. In a collectivistic society there is one huge corporation embracing the whole of the economy; its very size requires a complicated and rigid authoritarian and disciplinarian structure; planning cannot be disrupted by autonomous decisions reached by this or that branch of the economy, by one or another group of producers; there is no division of power. It is difficult to see how, under such conditions, the economy can be run on a basis other than that of total authority and total discipline. And if the economy and the state are one, how can this one thing act in an authoritarian way in its economic activities and act freely in its political activities? If the collectivist state is politically free, it is always possible that the slowness, vacillations, dissent, and neutralization of conflicting forces, which often characterize democratic procedure, will bring the economy to a standstill; if the efficiency of the economy is to be maintained, democratic procedure must be abolished—as has been done in the Soviet Union, in China, and in the so-called "People's Democracies."

Since the beginning of civilization, there have been numerous collectivist societies. Not a single one has enjoyed free institutions. Apart from its political aspects, collectivism is not conducive to the expression of individual autonomy. Because of the absence of private wealth, whatever the individual wishes to achieve can be achieved only through state authorization. No magazine can be printed unless the state provides the newsprint; no organization can have its headquarters unless the state provides the building; no meeting can be held unless the state provides the place. Miracles can happen; but it is wiser to believe in miracles (especially economic and political miracles) after they have happened, and not before. Meanwhile, it is well to note that in the Soviet Union and in the People's Democracies despotism and collectivism have gone together, that communists are satisfied with what they have achieved politically in the states they control, that for them a police state is the same as liberty: "Repression at home has become superfluous, because with the suppression of exploitation and the disappearance of exploiters, there was no one left to repress." [8]

[8] Stalin, quoted in *Contemporary Political Science* (Paris: UNESCO, 1950), p. 404.

Freedom usually brings with it differentiation and division. In a free society there are conservatives and radicals, believers and unbelievers, those who work hard and those who do not. Democracy, through the recognition of the legitimacy of differences and of opposition, implies a procedure through which these varied groups can live more or less peacefully together. The communist mind does not conceive differentiation, nor does it conceive the legitimacy of opposition. For the communist, what is different is either error or evil, and cannot be put on the same level as the truth represented by the communist idea. If communists were to be tolerant, their tolerance would be like that of the Ottoman Turks who allowed the "infidels" to survive but considered them subhuman. Communists maintain that the problems of opposition and "deviation" cannot arise in a truly socialistic society, because all citizens, being economically equal, will be of one mind. They do not consider that incomes may be equal but that functions will be different, or that there is no evidence that all members of an economic group react in the same way (in free societies property owners are divided, farmers are divided, workers are divided).

Whatever may have been their original intentions, Lenin and his collaborators proceeded to organize Russia on the basis of a totalitarian dictatorship. Dictatorships (more of an oligarchic type than the Russian one) have been organized in the countries in which communists have seized power during the last few years. Once an institution has been brought into existence, it is hard to kill it. Institutions often tend to develop according to a logic which has little or nothing to do with the concepts underlying them. There are very few instances of dictatorships ending of their own will. The end is usually the result of internal conflict or external attack; in the absence of either, dictatorships may last for centuries. If communist thinking included the autonomy of the individual, the control of the citizens over the government, the legitimacy of opposition, there would be a faint possibility of change. But these are the very ideas the communists have criticized most severely. It was their hatred for these ideas that induced them to cut themselves off from what had been until then the main stream of socialist thought.

It is possible to imagine that, having eliminated all opposition and dissent, communists might put an end to the use of the coercive powers of the state. It seems highly unlikely, however, that they will abandon the instruments required for the total enforcement of the communist will over the citizens. Were they to do so they would be no longer communists, but what they hate with the greatest passion: democratic socialists.

The "withering away" of the state is as out of the question as any minor "liberalization" in the organization of the movement, simply because any relaxation of political and intellectual pressure would bring into existence differences, deviations, and opposition, the legitimacy of which the communist mind cannot conceive. If communist societies continue to exist for some time, it is likely that they will evolve the institutions of self-perpetuating oligarchies (politburos or their equivalent) enforcing political tyranny, intellectual dogmatism, and economic monopoly.

After the seizure of political power, the main communist emphasis is on expansion of economic activities. Success will undoubtedly be achieved, thanks to the concentration of all available capital and of the direction of labor in the hands of a group with unlimited power. Results in the Soviet Union have been on the whole inferior to those achieved in capitalistic countries during the corresponding period of industrial expansion. The rate of economic expansion is not likely to increase, because the advantages of concentration and purposeful unified direction are offset by the repression of individual initiative and by bureaucracy. (In the United States the ratio of administrative workers to production workers is about 1 to 7; in the Soviet Union, 1 to 4; Soviet economic bureaucracy would fall into a morass of slowness, inefficiency, and waste unless held in line by exceptionally energetic individuals. But a bureaucratic society is not likely to produce many exceptionally energetic individuals.) For short periods the curve of economic expansion is likely to rise more in communist states than in countries with non-collectivistic economies. For longer periods (a decade or more), the opposite is likely to be true. The rate of economic expansion in communist states is important when we take into account their relations with non-communist states; it can however be considered relatively unimportant from the point of view of the internal strength of a communist state. Lacking the possibility of making comparisons, and unable to apply their critical faculties to the objective analysis of their conditions, citizens of communist states after a few years of dictatorship will believe whatever they are told by their leaders about the achievements of collectivism and its superiority over all other economic systems.

In the field of intellectual activities, the experience of communism is not likely to differ from that of other despotic societies. As long as there are minds formed in the pre-despotic period—where at least some liberty of thought was tolerated—a certain brilliancy may characterize mental developments. As generations go by, despotism gradually represses—sometimes to the point of suppression—the creativeness of the human mind, and intellectual stagnation and decadence follow. This process may be more rapid in a communist society than it has been in other authoritarian societies because (1) the communist conceptual framework (dialectical materialism) is a particularly narrow one, and because (2) means of thought control (particularly censorship and monopoly of education) are considerably more efficient in the twentieth century than they were in previous centuries. The curve indicating intellectual expression is likely to rise less and fall sooner than the curve of economic expansion.

Again on the basis of experiences made by other strongly authoritarian oligarchic states, it is legitimate to assume that, in spite of all efforts to enforce total conformity or orthodoxy, differences are likely to appear in the long run within the oligarchy, though not among the masses of citizens—or "subjects," as they should be called. Differences may arise on questions of principles or of policies, or simply on questions of personal interest. Often the greater the power, the more fierce is the struggle for power. To this must be added the economic incentive deriving from the fact that in a communist state political power is the best road to wealth, and that, as generations go by, the missionary spirit which at present is inspiring many communist leaders will be replaced more and more by materialistic considerations. In the European satellite states agreement is enforced by the all-powerful Politburo of the Soviet Union. But already in Yugoslavia the lack of control by the Soviet Politburo over the Yugoslav police has made it possible for Tito to "deviate." In China also the power is in the hands of a communist oligarchy autonomous vis-à-vis the Soviet one. A falling out of Chinese and Soviet communist leaders should not be expected in the near future, since the two groups are being held together by their common ideology and by strong common economic and political interests. But what is unlikely in the immediate future may not be an impossibility in the long run. In the Soviet Union itself there is no principle for the transfer of power; succession may be settled on the basis of an agreement among the members of the oligarchy. There will be occasions, however, when succession will have to be settled by force, and force may mean anything from a "palace revolution" to a civil war.

The present leaders of the communist states, from Mao to Rakosi, are mostly people endowed with strong personalities molded in a period of storm and stress. The younger leaders, as is already apparent in the Soviet Union, are as fanatic and bigoted as their elders, but their personalities are less impressive. They are the products of a highly bureaucratized society, and not of a hard struggle for survival in a competitive world. The qualities leading to communist success in a non-communist world are not the same as those leading to success within a communist society which demands servility, blind obedience, and absolute conformity. However dangerous it may be to prophesy, it is possible that, as time goes on, the quality of leadership of the communist societies will gradually deteriorate. Because in a totalitarian structure the impulse to action can only come from those who monopolize political power, their deterioration is likely to be reflected, in the long run, in the deterioration of communist institutions. Minds will stagnate, and so will all forms of individual and collective activities.

However vague and uncertain, a conclusion can be drawn from what has been stated in the last few paragraphs. Communism, as we have seen, is strong today. It may not be the strongest single movement existing in the world at the opening of the second half of the twentieth century, but it is certainly one of the strongest. Its strength derives mainly from a revulsion for conditions of suffering in which lived hundreds of millions of human beings in the Eastern Hemisphere. Once communism is on its own, the strength it derives from the defects of non-communist societies disappears. Because of its totalitarian structure, a communist state cannot produce the energy required to maintain fresh life in its institutions. It is therefore bound, if not to decay, certainly to stagnate. It is impossible to say how much time will be needed for this process to take place. But if non-communist states can—and there is no reason why they should not, unless seized by panic—hold their own for a generation or so, they are likely to be faced at the end of that period by a communism that has lost most of its present dynamic energy, a communism whose institutions are becoming empty and brittle shells, and whose leaders and followers, instead of being crusaders, have become mere bureaucrats.

If by *error* we mean engaging in action which gives different results from those expected, the communist leaders have already made a number of serious errors. Others can be expected. Three major and two minor past errors deserve mention. (1) In 1918 Lenin and his friends were convinced that within a few years all Europe would have gone communist; for five years, therefore, they engaged in revolutionary tactics which strengthened anti-communist forces. (2) In 1928 Stalin and the Comintern decided that the shortest cut to the triumph of communism in Europe was to help the authoritarian Right to destroy the main enemy—liberalism. The result was the sudden appearance of nazism, which proved to be stronger than either liberalism or communism, and which would have destroyed the Soviet Union if the latter had not been helped by what remained of liberal states. (3) In 1945 the Soviet Politburo was certain that an economic crisis would engulf the United States, and decided therefore on a policy of aggressiveness. The result was the strengthening of an anti-communist feeling in the United States and a greater resistance to Soviet expansion. Among the minor mistakes, (4) Tito was excommunicated on the assumption that the Yugoslav masses would revolt against him. (5) The Korean war was launched on the assumption that the United States would not fight. Through the concourse of favorable unforeseen happenings, none of the errors proved to be lethal to the communist movement. But what has been true for the past may not necessarily hold for the future.

Concerning its position in world affairs, we have seen that by the end of 1950 the communist movement exercised undisputed control over a large area of the Eastern Hemisphere, from the Bering Straits to Thuringia in central Germany, from the Arctic Ocean to the frontiers of Indochina, India, and the Near East. Over 750,000,000 people live in this area. If it is true, as contemporary events seem to bear out, that an efficient and dynamic dictatorship cannot be eliminated by the efforts of internal opposition, it is to be expected, in view of the lack of pressure from outside, that communism will remain the dominant political force in that area. Its weakening is likely to take place only after it has lost its dynamic energy—a process which, as we have seen, is not to be expected in the immediate future.

At the opposite extreme are the seven nations of the English-speaking world, where communism has achieved its least success. There we find conscious opposition to the monistic ideologies and to the totalitarian practices of communism, and a fairly clear vision of the fundamental differences between a free society and a servile one. In view of their high level of cultural, economic, and political developments, the English-speaking countries naturally play the main role in checking the advance of communism outside the areas where it has achieved success, thanks to chaotic conditions created by the two World Wars.

Communism is also still relatively weak where traditional oligarchies exercise political power over mainly passive masses of citizens, and where intellectuals are few and have relatively little influence. This is true, in varying degree, not only of most Latin American countries, but also of the Moslem world, of India, of parts of the southwestern Pacific area, and of Negro Africa. The weakening of these traditional oligarchies and the awakening of the masses of the people will lead to a crisis which will open the way to the development of new political forces. Communism there will certainly have the active support of the communist-controlled states. Democracy, in its individualistic-capitalistic form or in its limited socialistic-collectivistic form, should receive the support of the nations which operate within the framework of free institutions. Under present conditions it is difficult to foresee an overthrow of either the totalitarian form of government in the communist area, or of the democratic form of government in the English-speaking world. The influence of both communism and democracy in shaping the future of mankind is likely to depend to a great extent on their respective abilities to determine the changes which will occur among a majority of the population of the world in the second half of the twentieth century. If there are more than 750,000,000 inhabitants in the entire communist empire, there are only a little over 300,000,000 in the states in which free institutions are solidly entrenched: the English-speaking nations, France, the smaller European democracies, two or three Latin American states, etc. This leaves 1,200,000,000 people in the rest of the world. There is little doubt that the communist organizations are bracing themselves for the conquest of nations where democracy is shaky, and those nations which are only now emerging from their Middle Ages, as in the case of most Moslem countries, or are for the first time entering the world of civilization, as is the case of Negro Africa.

Whatever the importance of the attempts made to influence developments in the non-Western world, the main field of conflict at the middle of the century between the free or pluralistic form of society and the servile, monistic one, was represented by Continental western Europe. Because of the high level of cultural and economic activities, that section of Europe—in spite of the exhaustion caused by a succession of wars, civil wars, economic crises, and violent ideological conflicts—still plays an important role in world affairs. Nearly 250 million people live there, belonging to nations which only a generation ago were leading mankind, intellectually as well as politically and economically. They produce half as many goods and services as are produced in the whole of the communist world. If the human and material resources of Continental western Europe were to be controlled by the communists, they would come much closer to their realization of total triumph.

In that area there is probably a higher percentage of convinced fanatical communists than anywhere else. They can count on the support—varying from state to state—of anything between less than one tenth and nearly one third of the population. The majority of the people in France, Italy, Western Germany, and in the smaller states are definitely opposed to communism. This majority, however, is divided, and the various sections are considerably less dynamic than the communists. They often have a better understanding of what they do not want than of what they do want. Deep chasms separate the main anti-communist tendencies existing at present: Christian democracy (or Christian socialism), democratic socialism and liberalism (represented in various countries by several conflicting parties).[9] In parts of southern and central Europe fascism still appeals to large sections of the population. Wherever there are fascist or semi-fascist dictatorships, their non-communist opponents are often drawn within the orbit of communist influence.[10]

Without disparaging the courageous democratic opponents of communism who, since the end of World War II, have conducted a brilliant and on the whole successful fight against totalitarianism, we may assume that what will happen in Continental western Europe during the near future will be the result more of external pressures (American and Russian) than of the autonomous working of internal forces. National communist parties and underground communist military organizations enjoy the powerful backing of the Soviet Union which provides skilled organizers, trained leadership, clear-cut directives, asylum to those who need it, and probably financial means. Through the Marshall Plan and the North Atlantic Treaty Organization the United States has tried, in conjunction with other measures concerning individual European states, to strengthen anti-communist forces and to give them greater cohesion.

Begun as one of the many extreme tendencies unknown to the general public at the turn of the century, communism

[9] At the middle of 1951 there were thirteen states in Continental Europe in which the citizens could express their political will freely. Of the elected representatives of the people 36 percent belonged to Christian Democratic or similar parties, 27 percent to Democratic Socialist parties, and 17 percent to Liberal parties. The balance was made up by communists and by groups of the authoritarian Right.

[10] From a democratic point of view, one of the unfavorable aspects of the situation in many parts of non-Soviet Continental Europe is that the movement for checking communism can easily slide in the direction of unsavory Rightist totalitarianism. It happened in Italy in 1922 and in Germany in 1933, with tragic results for Europe and for the rest of mankind. It has happened in the Iberian peninsula; it may happen again in many countries. It is only in Switzerland, in the Scandinavian and in the Benelux states that democracy is as solidly entrenched as it is in the English-speaking world.

stands today as possibly the most powerful single political movement, if not in the world, certainly in most of the Eastern Hemisphere. Among the factors which have contributed to its success are:

1. the economic suffering of large sections of mankind;
2. the impression made by this suffering on Marxist intellectuals who form the solid core of the communist movement, and whose thinking is characterized by emotional postulates and extreme dogmatism;
3. the chaotic conditions in which many areas of Europe and Asia found themselves after the two World Wars, which enabled small minorities of well-organized and determined communists to seize political power;
4. the willingness to use brute force and to ignore every principle of ethics;
5. an uncompromising attitude which brooks no opposition and no deviation, and which gives to communism a cohesion and a homogeneity unknown to all other movements (except the fascist one); with this goes an internal structure which puts a maximum of power into the hands of a minimum of leaders;
6. the promise of the Millennium, coupled with a deep belief in the inevitability of socialism, and a remarkable spirit of sacrifice;
7. the ability of present communist leaders to adjust their action to ever-changing conditions; and
8. the power and prestige of the Soviet Union.

Communism today is less utopian than it was in its early revolutionary phase (1917-1923). It has a popular base which was lacking then; it enjoys the advantages of skilled and courageous leadership; it has become first and foremost a machine for the conquest of political power. There had been a beautiful dream, which is still the dream of many intellectuals who have little contact with reality. For those who believe in freedom, the reality of communism is a tragic one,[11] and it is no use deluding oneself that it will be transformed through an internal process of the communist movement.

Looking at the institutions of the communist state and of the communist parties, at what is and not at what should or might be, one cannot escape the conclusion that communism negates the noble attempt made during the last three hundred years in Western civilization to make liberty the basis of the social order, to evolve institutions through which continuous peaceful change can take place, to replace arbitrary rule with rule by law, and government by force with government by discussion. The attempt has produced but limited results so far; success can be achieved only through an effort which includes an uncompromising opposition to communism.

[11] "Communism, in its stage of so-called Utopia . . . taught love and kindness. . . . Upon becoming political . . . it turned to immorality, from love to hatred, the most intensified expression of which is Leninism." A. Gordin, *Communism Unmasked* (New York: Hord, 1940), p. 308. "An idea which has inspired whole generations to matchless heroism has become identified with the methods of a regime based on corruption, extortion and betrayal." Such is the revised opinion of the first secretary of the Comintern, A. Balabanova, *My Life as a Rebel* (New York: Harper, 1938), p. 319.

Bibliographical Note

BOOKS in English dealing with communism from a variety of angles are copious. Many of them are good, although the phenomenon is too new and stimulated the writers too deeply to allow them to describe and evaluate events and situations objectively. Students will find the following books useful, among others:

H. F. Armstrong, *Tito and Goliath* (New York: Macmillan, 1951). A keen analysis of Soviet-Yugoslav relations by one of the best-informed experts in international affairs. The book contains a detailed discussion of "Titoism," the one important heresy existing at the middle of the century.

F. Borkenau, *World Communism* (New York: Norton, 1939). Probably the best history of communism up to World War II which has appeared in the United States. The author had been close enough to communism to know it at first hand and, later, far enough removed to evaluate it without excessive bitterness.

E. Browder, *What Is Communism?* (New York: Vanguard Press, 1936). A former chairman of the Communist party of the United States describes communism to his fellow countrymen.

E. H. Carr, *The Bolshevik Revolution, 1917-1923* (New York: Macmillan, 1951). A British historian who has little sympathy for liberal democracy describes the Russian Revolution. There is only an appearance of objectivity. The book is valuable for the amount of information it contains but should be read in connection with other histories of the period.

Communism in Action (Washington: U. S. Government Printing Office, 1946). A very good summary of the position and the aims of communism as they could be seen by Americans immediately after the end of the war.

R. H. S. Crossman (ed.), *The God That Failed* (New York: Harper, 1950). A useful anthology of the intellectual crisis undergone by six former communists and fellow travelers.

D. Y. Dallin, *The Real Soviet Russia* (New Haven: Yale University Press, 1944). A good analysis of conditions in Russia after twenty-five years of communist regime. The author successfully makes facts speak instead of emotions.

M. Ebon, *World Communism Today* (New York: Whittlesey, 1948). Definitely inferior to the book by Borkenau. Useful, however, because it includes considerable information on the developments of communism after 1939.

History of the Communist Party in the Soviet Union (New York: International Publishers, 1939). It presents the official Stalinist interpretation.

A. Koestler, *Darkness at Noon* (New York: Macmillan, 1941). A novel, but a valuable book for the understanding of the communist mind and of the way it works. (This understanding is probably as important as the knowledge of the industrial strength of the Soviet Empire.)

Mao Tse-tung, *China's New Democracy* (New York: New Century Publishers, 1945). The gospel of the fifth prophet at present acknowledged by the communists. Of fundamental importance for an understanding of the developments of China under communist rule.

J. Oneal and G. A. Werner, *American Communism* (New York: Dutton, 1947). Two critics who know it well describe the communist movement of the United States.

B. Schwartz, *Chinese Communism and The Rise of Mao* (Cambridge: Harvard University Press, 1951). When dealing with communism in the Far East, knowledge is usually less than in the case of Russian or Western communism, and emotionalism even higher. Good books are extremely rare. This is one of them.

J. Stalin, *Leninism, Selected Writings* (New York: International Publishers, 1942). The fourth prophet interprets the third.

B. D. Wolfe, *Three Who Made a Revolution* (New York: Dial, 1948). A good account of the lives, aspirations, and activities of Lenin, Trotsky, and Stalin.

The case for communism has been made by Lenin and Stalin in a number of works which have been only partially translated in English. Among those available to the American public, written by other communists and sympathizers, the following can be consulted profitably: N. I. Bukharin, *The ABC of Communism* (Glasgow: Socialist Labour Press, 1921); E. Burns, *Russia's Productive System* (New York: Dutton, 1931); M. H. Dobb, *Soviet Economic Development since 1917* (New York: International Publishers, 1948); R. P. Dutt, *Fascism and Social Revolution* (New York: International Publishers, 1935); W. Z. Foster, *Towards Soviet America* (New York: Coward-McCann, 1932); W. Gallacher, *The Case for Communism* (Harmondsworth: Penguin Books, 1949); H. Johnson, *The Soviet Power* (New York: International Publishers, 1940); Karl Marx, *Capital, The Communist Manifesto, and Other Writings* (New York: Modern Library, 1932); S. Spender, *Forward from Liberalism* (New York: Random House, 1937); J. Strachey, *The Coming Struggle for Power* (New York: Covici, Friede, 1933); A. L. Strong, *This Soviet World* (New York: Holt, 1936); and S. J. Webb and B. Webb, *Soviet Communism: A New Civilization?* (London: Longmans, Green, 1935).

The case against communism has been made by authors who have never been communists and, probably as effectively if not more effectively, by many others who have been communists or fellow travelers. Among their works are: A. Balabanova, *My Life as a Rebel* (New York: Harper, 1938); A. Barmine, *One Who Survived* (New York: Putnam, 1945); L. F. Budenz, *Men without Faces; The Communist Conspiracy* (New York: Harper, 1950); J. Burnham, *The Coming Defeat of Communism* (New York: Day, 1950); W. H. Chamberlin, *Russia's Iron Age* (Boston: Little, Brown, 1934); and *Blueprint for World Conquest, as Outlined by the Communist International* (Chicago: Human Events, 1946); D. Y. Dallin and B. I. Nicolaevsky, *Forced Labor in the Soviet Union* (New Haven: Yale University Press, 1947); R. Fisher, *Stalin and German Communism* (Cambridge: Harvard University Press, 1948); A. P. G. Gide, *Return from the USSR* (New York: Knopf, 1937); K. Kautsky, *Social Democracy versus Communism* (New York: Rand School Press, 1946); A. Koestler, *The Yogi and the Commissar* (New York: Macmillan, 1945), and several other books by the same author; V. A. Kravchenko, *I Chose Freedom* (New York: Scribner's, 1946); E. Lyons, *Assignment in Utopia* (New York: Harcourt, Brace, 1937); A. Rossi, *A Communist Party in Action* (New Haven: Yale University Press, 1949); B. Souvarine, *Stalin, A Critical Survey of Bolshevism* (New York: Longmans, Green, 1939); and F. Utley, *The Dream We Lost, Soviet Russia Then and Now* (New York: Day, 1940).

Among the books which try to discuss Russian communism without passion, are: N. Berdyaev, *The Origin of Russian Communism* (London: 1937); S. N. Harper, *The Russia I Believe In* (Chicago: University of Chicago Press, 1945); H. Kelsen, *The Political Theory of Bolshevism* (Berkeley: University of California Press, 1948); R. Schlesinger, *The Spirit of Post-War Russia: Soviet Ideology 1917-1946* (London: Dobson, 1947). On Western communism one should read Einaudi, Domenach and Garosci, *Communism in Western Europe* (Ithaca: Cornell University Press, 1951).

On Lenin, one can read D. Shub, *Lenin, A Biography* (New York: Doubleday, 1948); on Stalin, I. Deutscher, *Stalin, A Political Biography* (New York: Oxford University Press, 1949). On the Russian Revolution, besides the works already mentioned on pages 109-110: W. H. Chamberlin, *The Russian Revolution 1917-1921* (New York: Macmillan, 1935); V. Chernov, *The Great Russian Revolution* (New Haven: Yale University Press, 1936); A. F. Kerenski, *The Catastrophe* (New York: Appleton, 1921); P. N. Miliukov, *Russia To-day and To-morrow* (New York: Macmillan, 1922); N. Lenin, *The Revolution of 1917* and *Towards the Seizure of Power* (New York: International Publishers, 1929 and 1932); and L. Trotsky, *The History of the Russian Revolution* (New York: Simon and Schuster, 1936).

Index